INTERNATIONAL ACCLAIM FOR PROFESSOR M.S. RAO'S BOOK!

"Professor M.S. Rao continues to help all employees, from leaders to new employees, find meaning and purpose from work. He explores timeless spiritual principles that permeate all major religions and translates them into specific daily practices that will create a meaningful work environment."

Dave Ulrich
Rensis Likert Professor, Ross School of Business,
University of Michigan Partner, the RBL Group

"The first step on any leadership journey is toward an exploration of the inner territory. With 'See the Light in You' Professor M.S. Rao brightly illuminates the pathways to greater personal awareness and awakening. Combining ancient wisdom from spiritual teachers with his contemporary insights and observations, Professor Rao offers the reader a field guide for the soul."

Jim Kouzes,
Coauthor of The Leadership Challenge and Executive Fellow of
Leadership, Leavey School of Business, Santa Clara University

"Professor M.S. Rao is recognized as the Father of Soft Leadership. In his latest book, he illuminates how spirituality suffuses effective leadership, and renders it compatible with integrating life and work."

James Strock,
Author, Serve to Lead

"This book is powerful, enlightening and uplifting. If you are looking for career advice or searching for meaning in your life, use this book as your compass. It is thought-provoking and provides a wealth of actionable advice. Professor M.S. Rao has a stellar reputation for being one of the most important thought leaders of our time. This book clearly demonstrates why he deserves that distinction. I strongly recommend it."

Frank Sonnenberg
Award-winning author of six books, including:
Follow Your Conscience and Managing with a Conscience

"In this book, Professor M S Rao, the International Management Thinker explores spiritual leadership and life leadership. He implores you to follow the philosophy of 'health first, education second, and wealth third' to lead a happy and meaningful life. I strongly recommend reading this book."

Terri Levine,
Best-selling author of Turbocharge How To Transform
Your Business As A Heartrepreneur

SEE THE LIGHT IN YOU

Acquire Spiritual Powers to Achieve Mindfulness, Wellness, Happiness, and Success

PROFESSOR M.S. RAO

Waterside Productions

First Printing, 2020

ISBN-13: 978-1-949003-13-0 print edition
ISBN-13: 978-1-949003-14-7 ebook edition

Waterside Productions
2055 Oxford Ave
Cardiff, CA 92007
www.waterside.com

Dedicated to Sri Muppavarapu Venkaiah Naidu, the Honourable Vice President of India—A gifted orator and leader.

TABLE OF CONTENTS

See the Light in You: Acquire Spiritual Powers to Achieve Mindfulness, Wellness, Happiness, and Success

SPIRITUAL STROKES

"Be a lamp to yourself. Be your own confidence. Hold on to the truth within yourself as to the only truth." — Buddha

"What you think, you become. What you feel, you attract. What you imagine, you create." — Buddha

"Neither fire nor wind, birth nor death can erase our good deeds" — Buddha

"Meditation brings wisdom; lack of meditation leaves ignorance. Know well what leads you forward and what holds you back, and choose the path that leads to wisdom." — Buddha

"Your body is precious. It is our vehicle for awakening. Treat it with care." — Buddha

"To understand everything is to forgive everything." — Buddha

"Do not dwell in the past, do not dream of the future, concentrate the mind on the present moment." — Buddha

"Purity of speech, of the mind, of the senses, and of a compassionate heart are needed by one who desires to rise to the divine platform." — Chanakya

"Knowing yourself is the beginning of all wisdom." — Aristotle

"You cannot travel the path until you have become the path itself." — Buddha

"The beauty of the soul shines out when a man bears with composure one heavy mischance after another, not because he does not feel them, but because he is a man of high and heroic temper." — Aristotle

"Our prime purpose in this life is to help others. And if you can't help them, at least don't hurt them." — Dalai Lama XIV

"One's everyday life is never capable of being separated from his spiritual being." — Mahatma Gandhi

"Darkness cannot drive out darkness; only light can do that. Hate cannot drive out hate; only love can do that." — Martin Luther King, Jr.

"The tears of faithfulness to your beliefs cleanse your spirit to envision the road ahead. Everything is possible for the person who believes." — Adlin Sinclair

"A book must be an ice-axe to break the seas frozen inside our soul." — Franz Kafka

"I'm doing my best to be mindful about how I'm living: to be kind and patient, and not to impose a bad mood on somebody else. Being mindful is as good a way to be spiritual as anything else." — Deirdre O'Kane

"A spiritual partnership is between people who promise themselves to use all of their experiences to grow spiritually. They use their emotions to show them how to create constructive and healthy and joyful consequences instead of destructive and unhealthy and painful consequences." — Gary Zukav

"A life is either all spiritual or not spiritual at all. No man can serve two masters. Your life is shaped by the end you live for. You are made in the image of what you desire." — Thomas Merton

"I am a spiritual person in an eastern religion kind of way. I learned that happiness for all of us is a switch that you flick in your brain. It doesn't have anything to do with getting a new house, a new car, a new girlfriend, or a new pair of shoes. Our culture is very much about that; we are never happy with what we have today." — Tom Ford

"Business underlies everything in our national life, including our spiritual life. Witness the fact that in the Lord's Prayer, the first petition is for daily bread. No one can worship God or love his neighbor on an empty stomach." — Woodrow Wilson

"It is indeed a radical act of love just to sit down and be quiet for a time by yourself." — Jon Kabat Zinn

"Choosing to be positive and having a grateful attitude is going to determine how you're going to live your life." — Joel Osteen

"Why don't you start believing that no matter what you have or haven't done, that your best days are still out in front of you." — Joel Osteen

"God wants us to prosper financially, to have plenty of money, to fulfill the destiny He has laid out for us." — Joel Osteen

"Your own Self-realization is the greatest service you can render the world." — Ramana Maharshi

"No one succeeds without effort... Those who succeed owe their success to perseverance." — Ramana Maharshi

"The degree of freedom from unwanted thoughts and the degree of concentration on a single thought are the measures to gauge spiritual progress." — Ramana Maharshi

"No country can be great if even a small minority in the country feels neglected." — Sri Ravi Shankar

"Books are uniquely portable magic." — Stephen King

"If there is a void in your life then you will never fill it with cash!" — Stephen Richards

"We thus arrive at a conception of the relation of science to religion very different from the usual one … I maintain that the cosmic religious feeling is the strongest and noblest motive for scientific research." — Albert Einstein

"We have created a manic world nauseous with the pursuit of material wealth. Many also bear their cross of imagined deprivation, while their fellow human beings remain paralyzed by real poverty. We drown in the thick sweetness of our sensual excess, and our shameless opulence, while our discontent souls suffocate in the arid wasteland of spiritual deprivation." — Anthon St. Maarten

"In war, the strong make slaves of the weak, and in peace, the rich make slaves of the poor." — Oscar Wilde

"[My father] loved me tenderly and shyly from a distance, and later on took a naive pride in seeing my name in print." — Arthur Koestler

"One is worthy as a son when he removes all his father's troubles." — Dada Bhagwan

"Nothing is given to man on earth – struggle is built into the nature of life, and conflict is possible – the hero is the man who lets no obstacle prevent him from pursuing the values he has chosen." — Andrew Bernstein

"A single conversation across the table with a wise man is worth a month's study of books." — Chinese Proverb

"I alone cannot change the world, but I can cast a stone across the water to create many ripples." — Mother Teresa

"Strength does not come from winning. Your struggles develop your strengths. When you go through hardships and decide not to surrender, that is strength." — Arnold Schwarzenegger

"Reading makes a full man, meditation a profound man, discourse a clear man." — Benjamin Franklin

"When things are going good the business grows when things are going bad, you grow." — Chinese proverb

"It's time to start living the life you've imagined." — Henry James

"Imagination is everything. It is the preview of life's coming attractions." — Albert Einstein

"Writing is an escape from a world that crowds me. I like being alone in a room. It's almost a form of meditation – an investigation of my own life." — Neil Simon

"Thoughts lead on to purposes; purposes go forth in action; actions form habits; habits decide character; and character fixes our destiny." — Tryon Edwards

"You will get all you want in life if you help enough other people get what they want." — Zig Ziglar

"The life of the dead is placed in the memory of the living." — Marcus Tullius Cicero

"The best vision is insight." — Malcolm S. Forbes

"Place a higher priority on discovering what a win looks like for the other person." — Harvey Robbins

"It is obvious that we can no more explain a passion to a person who has never experienced it than we can explain light to the blind." — T.S. Elliot

"We are using at most 5% of the potential of the human mind. 100% human potential is the result of proper education. So imagine a world where people are using their full mental and emotional potential." — John Hagelin

"What material success does is provide you with the ability to concentrate on other things that really matter. And that is being able to make a difference, not only in your own life but in other people's lives." — Oprah Winfrey

"The ultimate value of life depends upon awareness and the power of contemplation rather than upon mere survival." — Aristotle

"Life is a rough biography. Memories smooth out the edges." — Terri Guillemets

"First they ignore you, then they laugh at you, then they fight you, then you win." — Mahatma Gandhi

"The art of living lies not in eliminating but in growing with troubles." — Bernard Baruch

"A man will fight harder for his interests than for his rights." — Napoleon Bonaparte

"I believe there's an inner power that makes winners or losers. And the winners are the ones who really listen to the truth of their hearts." — Sylvester Stallone

"The life that conquers is the life that moves with a steady resolution and persistence toward a predetermined goal. Those who succeed are those who have thoroughly learned the immense importance of plan in life, and the tragic brevity of time." — W.J. Davison

"Tenderness and kindness are not signs of weakness and despair, but manifestations of strength and resolution." — Kahil Gibran

"Trust men and they will be true to you: treat them greatly and they will show themselves great." — Ralph Waldo Emerson

"More than ninety-five percent of your brain activity, as you consciously read this sentence, is being used by your subconscious mind." — Kevin Michel, *Moving Through Parallel Worlds To Achieve Your Dreams*

"In every human endeavor, there are two arenas of engagement: the outer and the inner. The outer game is played on an external arena to overcome external obstacles to reach an external goal. The inner game takes place within the mind of the player and is played against such obstacles as fear, self-doubt, lapses in focus, and limiting concepts or assumptions. The inner game is played to overcome the self-imposed obstacles that prevent an individual or team from accessing their full potential." — Timothy Gallwey

"The best kind of happiness is a habit you're passionate about." — Shannon L. Alder

"Habits are formed by the repetition of particular acts. They are strengthened by an increase in the number of repeated acts. Habits are also weakened or broken, and contrary habits are formed by the repetition of contrary acts." — Mortimer J. Adler

"Success is a few simple disciplines, practiced every day; while failure is simply a few errors in judgment, repeated every day." — Jim Rohn

"The way we talk to our children becomes their inner voice." — Peggy O'Mara

"To visualize is to see what is not there, what is not real — a dream. To visualize is, in fact, to make visual lies. Visual lies, however, have a way of coming true." — Peter McWilliams

"Having a vision for your life allows you to live out of hope, rather than out of your fears." — Stedman Graham

"The life and love we create is the life and love we live." — Leo Buscaglia

"There are two ways of spreading light: to be the candle or the mirror that reflects it." — Edith Wharton

"I never knew a man come to greatness or eminence who lay abed late in the morning." — Johnathan Swift

"Those who think they have not time for bodily exercise will sooner or later have to find time for illness." — Edward Stanley

"Just as you wouldn't leave the house without taking a shower, you shouldn't start the day without at least 10 minutes of sacred practice: prayer, meditation, inspirational reading." — Marianne Williamson

"Meditation is difficult for many people because their thoughts are always on some distant object or place. One form of meditation is to label the thought as it appears and then choose to let it go." — Wayne Dyer

"I get up at an unholy hour in the morning my workday is completed by the time the sun rises. I have a slightly bad back which has made an enormous contribution to American literature." — David Eddings

"It is easier to find men who will volunteer to die, than to find those who are willing to endure pain with patience." — Julius Caesar

"Health is not a mere absence of disease. It is a dynamic expression of life – in terms of how joyful, loving and enthusiastic you are." — Sri Sri Ravi Shankar

"Mindfulness helps you go home to the present. And every time you go there and recognize a condition of happiness that you have, happiness comes." — Thich Nhat Hanh

"Our bodies are our gardens to which our wills are gardeners." — William Shakespeare

"It seems, in fact, as though the second half of a man's life is made up of nothing but the habits he has accumulated during the first half." — Fyodor Dostoyevsky

"Patience, persistence and perspiration make an unbeatable combination for success." — Napoleon Hill

"I've had a lot of worries in my life, most of which never happened." — Mark Twain

"Before this generation loses wisdom, one advice – read books." — Amit Kalantri

"Books are lighthouses erected in the great sea of time." — E.P. Whipple

"If we encounter a man of rare intellect, we should ask him what books he reads." — Ralph Waldo Emerson

"The great use of life is to spend it for something that outlasts it." — William James

"For a person who is not aware that he is doing anything wrong has no desire to be put right. You have to catch yourself doing it before you can reform." — Seneca

"We have self-centered minds which get us into plenty of trouble. If we do not come to understand the error in the way we think, our self-awareness, which is our greatest blessing, is also our downfall." — Joko Beck

"As soon as you honor the present moment, all unhappiness and struggle dissolve, and life begins to flow with joy and ease. When you act out the present-moment awareness, whatever you do becomes imbued with a sense of quality, care, and love – even the most simple action." — Eckhart Tolle

"Success in any endeavor requires single-minded attention to detail and total concentration." — Willie Sutton

"All good is gained by those whose thought and life are kept pointed close to one main thing, not scattered abroad upon a thousand." — Stephen McKenna

"The more intensely we feel about an idea or a goal, the more assuredly the idea, buried deep in our subconscious, will direct us along the path to its fulfillment." — Earl Nightingale

"The degree of freedom from unwanted thoughts and the degree of concentration on a single thought are the measures to gauge spiritual progress." — Ramana Maharshi

"Practice meditation regularly. Meditation leads to eternal bliss. Therefore meditate, meditate." — Swami Sivananda

"Happiness is your nature. It is not wrong to desire it. What is wrong is seeking it outside when it is inside." — Ramana Maharshi

"In today's rush, we all think too much — seek too much — want too much — and forget about the joy of just being." — Eckhart Tolle

"The most precious gift we can offer others is our presence. When mindfulness embraces those we love, they will bloom like flowers." — Thich Nhat Hanh

"We are awakened to the profound realization that the true path to liberation is to let go of everything." — Jack Kornfield

"He who does not know how to look back at where he came from will never get to his destination." — Jose Rizal

"It is my right to be rich, happy, and successful. Money flows to me freely, copiously, and endlessly. I am forever conscious of my true worth. I give of my talents freely, and I am wonderfully blessed financially. It is wonderful!" — Joseph Murphy

"It is psychological law that whatever we desire to accomplish we must impress upon the subjective or subconscious mind." — Orison Swett Marden

"The possibilities of creative effort connected with the subconscious mind are stupendous and imponderable. They inspire one with awe." — Napoleon Hill

"A leader is one who can clearly communicate a vision and motivate others to action ... one who discovers and maintains a lifelong pursuit of God's truths to positively impact individuals and the world." — Bruce E. Winston

"Everyone has in him something divine, something his own, a chance of perfection and strength in however small a sphere which God offers him to take or refuse. The task is to find it, develop it & use it. The chief aim of education should be to help the growing soul to draw out that in itself which is best and make it perfect for a noble use." — Sri Aurobindo

"Yoga does not remove us from the reality or responsibilities of everyday life but rather places our feet firmly and resolutely in the practical ground of experience. We don't transcend our lives; we return to the life we left behind in the hopes of something better." — Donna Farhi

"In spite of illness, in spite even of the archenemy sorrow, one can remain alive long past the usual date of disintegration if one is unafraid of change, insatiable in intellectual curiosity, interested in big things, and happy in small ways." — Edith Wharton

"You have to grow from the inside out. None can teach you, none can make you spiritual. There is no other teacher but your own soul." — Swami Vivekananda

"My hope of the future lies in the youths of character, intelligent, renouncing all for the service of others, and obedient – good to themselves and the country at large." — Swami Vivekananda

"Neither money pays, nor name pays, nor fame, nor learning; it is CHARACTER that cleaves through adamantine walls of difference." — Swami Vivekananda

"Man is least himself when he talks in his own person. Give him a mask, and he will tell you the truth." — Oscar Wilde

"To be nobody but myself-in a world which is doing its best, night and day, to make me somebody else-means to fight the hardest battle any human can fight, and never stop fighting." — E.E. Cummings

"You will not be punished for your anger, you will be punished by your anger." — Buddha

"Anger is just a cowardly extension of sadness. It's a lot easier to be angry at someone than it is to tell them you're hurt." — Tom Gates

"Never forget what a man says to you when he is angry." — Henry Ward Beecher

"Fatigue, discomfort, discouragement are merely symptoms of effort." — Morgan Freeman

"If you wait for the mango fruits to fall, you'd be wasting your time while others are learning how to climb the tree." — Michael Bassey Johnson, *Master of Maxims*

"Comparison is the thief of joy." — Theodore Roosevelt

"Why compare yourself to others? You never know what people endured to get where they are." — Lailah Gifty Akita

"On the relationship side, if you teach people to respond actively and constructively when someone they care about has a victory, it increases love and friendship and decreases the probability of depression." — Martin Seligman

"It's a recession when your neighbor loses his job; it's a depression when you lose yours." — Harry S Truman

"Dirty hands, feet, and body, can be washed clean with water; Soiled clothes washed clean with soap; But when the mind becomes dark with sin, Divine love alone can restore it to purity." — Guru Nanak

"When the body aches, the soul too is weakened and one is unable to pray properly; even when clear of sins. Thus you must guard the health of the body carefully." — Baal Shem Tov

"You have to grow from the inside out. None can teach you, none can make you spiritual. There is no other teacher but your own soul." — Swami Vivekananda

"Never respect men merely for their riches, but rather for their philanthropy; we do not value the sun for its height, but for its use." — Gamaliel Bailey

"Philanthropy and social change work are at their best when they are driven by your values and connected to what you care about most." — Charles Bronfman

"Life's persistent and most urgent question is 'What are you doing for others?'" — Martin Luther King Jr.

"The test of a civilization is in the way that it cares for its helpless members." — Pearl S. Buck

"If you want to end the war then instead of sending guns, send books. Instead of sending tanks, send pens. Instead of sending soldiers, send teachers." — Malala Yousafzai

"For Achilles, the death of Patroclus pushed him into a fury, but it was not only grief that drove him. It was also a sense of shame and guilt because he had not been there to protect his friend. Sometimes men in combat feel this sort of survivor's guilt even though, realistically, they could have done nothing to prevent their comrade's death." — Nel Noddings, *Peace Education: How We Come to Love and Hate War*

"Hatred paralyzes life; love releases it. Hatred confuses life; love harmonizes it. Hatred darkens life; love illuminates it." — Martin Luther King, Jr.

"Anxiety is the illness of our age. We worry about ourselves, our family, our friends, our work, and our state of the world. If we allow worry to fill our hearts, sooner or later we will get sick." — Thich Nhat Hanh

"We must accept finite disappointment, but never lose infinite hope." — Martin Luther King, Jr.

"The unexamined life is not worth living." — Socrates

"Religion survives because it answers three questions that every reflective person must ask. Who am I? Why am I here? How then shall I live?" — Jonathan Sacks

"All life is an experiment. The more experiments you make, the better." — Ralph Waldo Emerson

"The doctor of the future will give no medication, but will interest his patients in the care of the human frame, diet and in the cause and prevention of disease." — Thomas A. Edison

"When we look at nutrition from a purely scientific point of view, there is no place for consciousness. And yet, consciousness could be one of the crucial determinants of the metabolism of the food itself." — Deepak Chopra., M.D.

"There is no greater sickness in the world today than the lack of love." — Mother Teresa

"Spiritual values transcend the material artifacts that we can touch and see. They take us into the realm of beauty, inspiration, and love." — Nido Qubein

"The bargain was this: Admit the anxiety as an essential part of yourself and in exchange that anxiety will be converted into energy, unstable but manageable. Stop with the self-flagellating and become yourself, with scars and tics." — Daniel Smith, *Monkey Mind: A Memoir of Anxiety*

"Guilt at least has a purpose; it tells us we've violated some ethical code. Ditto for remorse. Those feelings are educational; they manufacture wisdom. But regret—regret is useless." — Daniel Smith, *Monkey Mind: A Memoir of Anxiety*

"Mindfulness and Emotional Intelligence both emphasize people's abilities to perceive, understand and regulate their thoughts and emotions." — John Darwin

"The longest journey you will ever take is the eighteen inches from your head to your heart." — Thich Nhat Hanh

"What you resist, persists." — Carl Gustav Jung

"Whatever is begun in anger, ends in shame." — Benjamin Franklin

"My mission in life is not merely to survive, but to thrive; and to do so with some passion, some compassion, some humor, and some style." — Maya Angelou

"Despite how open, peaceful, and loving you attempt to be, people can only meet you as deeply as they've met themselves." — Matt Kahn

"Two things to remember in life: Take care of your thoughts when you are alone and take care of your words when you are with people." — Unknown

"It's only when we truly know and understand that we have a limited time on earth — and that we have no way of knowing when our time is up — that we will begin to live each day to the fullest as if it was the only one we had." — Elisabeth Kübler-Ross

"You have power over your mind—not outside events. Realize this, and you will find strength." — Marcus Aurelius

"Your sacred space is where you can find yourself again and again." — Joseph Campbell

"We should start choosing our thoughts like we choose our clothes for the day." —Farnoosh Brock

"We take care of the future best by taking care of the present now." — Jon Kabat-Zinn

"You, yourself, as much as anybody in the entire universe, deserve your love and affection." — Buddha

FOREWORD

While we see many positive things around the world, it is a fact that there are also problems that we as humans face in life. Many of them are manmade, and could be solved or reduced by dealing with them positively. All major religious traditions that adhere to a philosophy provide explanations and ways to overcome many of our predicaments or sad experiences in life.

At a personal level, when faced with such events, I find the ancient Indian tradition of mind training very effective. However, I am sure that there are many others who may not feel any inclination towards such a tradition. Nevertheless, the fact still remains that for their numerous problems, people still need some form of solution that would suit their mental dispositions.

Professor M. S. Rao's book *See the Light in You* contains practical advice that would be useful for individuals in leading their lives sensibly. It is my belief and conviction that if we live our lives with respect for others' wellbeing and put more emphasis on the peace of mind than on material values, we will become happier. I am sure readers of this book will find it interesting and helpful in leading a happy and meaningful life.

26 May 2017

PREFACE

"Just as a candle cannot burn without fire, men cannot live without a spiritual life." —Buddha

Welcome to *See the Light in You: Acquire Spiritual Powers to Achieve Mindfulness, Wellness, Happiness, and Success.* You must be surprised to see another book on leadership. This book is on spiritual leadership which is the need of the hour in the current complex world. It underscores mindfulness, wellness, happiness and leadership success. It addresses anxiety, depression, fatigue and other health hazards arising from technology. It outlines inspiring stories to add value to society and make a difference in the world. It emphasizes to enjoy little things in daily life to make your life a memorable one. It highlights moral education and philanthropy. It concludes to emphasize health first, education second, and wealth third to lead a successful and meaningful life. I hope this book will inspire you to lead your life with purpose and meaning.

Professor M. S. Rao, Ph.D.

.

ACKNOWLEDGMENTS

Writing a book is never a solo project. I am deeply indebted to many people whose expertise, wisdom and encouragement kept me going. My wife's encouragement made this book possible. My wife, Padmavathy, is a symbol of sacrifice and support for my books and is also an immeasurable blessing in my life.

I thank everyone including the team of Waterside Productions, Inc for publication of this book. I specifically thank Bill Gladstone, Josh Freel and Ken Fraser for their initiative, commitment, positive attitude and professionalism in the publication of this book. I thank all those behind the scenes – editors, production staff, and copyeditors – who have helped bring this work to life.

I would like to thank my coaching clients, who are among the most fantastic leaders. I have learned far more from them than they have learned from me.

I express special thanks to all my readers who graciously took time off from their busy schedules to write to me, share their views, and offer feedback on my books.

1 – LEAD YOUR LIFE SPIRITUALLY

"If you light a lamp for somebody, it will also brighten your path." —Buddha

People encounter several challenges globally due to various reasons such as volatility, uncertainty, complexity, and ambiguity. Currently, they encounter challenges much bigger than their predecessors due to rapid growth in technology. They enjoy more comforts than their predecessors but suffer from ailments arising from stress and burnout. Hence, the importance of spiritualism is felt more than ever before. In this introductory chapter, we will discuss spiritualism that helps you lead your personal, professional and social life happily.

What is Spiritualism?

"Spiritual relationship is far more precious than physical. Physical relationship divorced from spiritual is body without soul." —Mahatma Gandhi

Spiritualism is more about invisible than visible. It is more about the mind and human spirit than the so-called materialistic things. It is not connected with any religion. Spiritualism is a way of life anyone can practice achieving harmony, peace, and love in life.

Spiritualism is a means to achieve your end of salvation. Spiritualism synchronizes your mind and body with the soul. Spiritualism is to surrender yourself to serve others. It is to refine your thought process to build a positive attitude and develop an attitude of gratitude. It is to keep people around you happy and warm with your positive thoughts and vibrations. It is to build better communities and societies. It is to build a better world. Above all, it is to leave a better legacy to the next generations.

It is observed that the people who are divorced, bankrupt and encounter death in their family become more spiritualistic. They find solace in spiritualism since they forget their unpleasant events and failures.

Advantages of Spiritualism

There are innumerable advantages associated with spiritualism. You develop open-mindedness and appreciate others' achievements. You become tolerant, patient, optimist, confident and compassionate. You maintain the sound mind in a healthy body. You enjoy every moment of your life.

Spiritualism helps forgive others and forget the unpleasant past. It helps look at similarities, not differences. It breaks barriers and builds bridges. It connects people and brings them into one platform. It improves health and ensures longevity. It helps overcome challenges with calm and composure. It helps make smart and wise decisions by blending the head, heart, and gut. It converts you into a better human being.

Spiritualism enlightens people. It helps them introspect themselves and empathize with others. It eliminates conflicts and enhances unity and camaraderie. It removes negative thoughts from their mind and replaces with positive thoughts. It enhances their creativity and helps them think differently. It helps them realize and unlock their hidden potential. Above all, it helps them find meaning in their lives to make a difference to the world.

The human brain is basically rewired to ensure survival rather than success. We spend most of our time with repetitive thoughts. And most of our thoughts are negative in nature. Research shows that the average person spends 95% of their day going through repeat thoughts. Worse, an average 75% are repeat negative things, just 20% on positive repeat thoughts and only a tiny 5% on new ideas.

When you stress on spiritualism you think positively without wasting your time on your unpleasant past events. You emphasize new areas and explore them to achieve amazing success and happiness.

Spiritualistic versus Materialistic People

> "It is the spiritual always which determines the material."
> —Thomas Carlyle

The materialistic people crave for money while the spiritualistic people crave for love, peace, and happiness. For materialistic people, money is the end while for spiritualistic people, peace is the end. Hence, their goals are different. William James rightly differentiated, "Materialism means simply the denial that the moral order is eternal, and the cutting off of ultimate hopes; spiritualism means the affirmation of eternal moral order and the letting loose of hope." Technology has added further woes to complexity. In fact, technology is a double-edged sword. It is both a boon and bane. It is boon because it brought comforts to the humankind. It is bane because it increased the health complications by replacing spiritualism with materialism.

A Blueprint to Lead Your Spiritual Life

Fela Kuti remarked, "To be spiritual is not by praying and going to church. Spiritualism is the understanding of the universe so that it can be a better place to live in." Here are some tips to lead your spiritual life. Be simple and humble. Walk your talk. Be a giver, not a taker. Invest some time regularly to serve others. Associate with positive and likeminded people. Emphasize ideas rather than individuals and issues. Add value to others.

The Body is Mortal and Soul is Immortal

> "He who loves, never grows old. God is a shining example."
> —Sri Chinmoy

The human body undergoes three phases—creation, generation, and destruction. The body is mortal while the soul is immortal. To make our lives immortal, it is advisable to wed spiritualism.

When a man marries a woman, he craves for physical unification first, emotional unification second and spiritual unification third. When a married couple understands each other well, they reach the third stage successfully. It is possible only when people understand and appreciate spiritualism.

Love Your Mother but don't Hate another Person's Mother

Love your mother but don't hate another person's mother. As your mother is precious to you, another person's mother is equally precious to him/her. As your race, religion, region, language, ethnicity, culture, and community are precious to you; they are equally precious to others.

People must empathize with others to make a difference in the lives of others. We need empathetic leaders like Mahatma Gandhi, Martin Luther King Jr, Mother Teresa, Nelson Mandela, Mikhail Gorbachev, and Dalai Lama; and religious leaders like Jesus, Buddha, Muhammad and Gurunanak to name a few to achieve global peace, prosperity, stability and security. Remember, what Mother Teresa said when asked what you can do to promote world peace: "Go home and love your family." As charity begins at home, let us promote global peace by loving our families and empathizing with others first.

Life is an Echo

"Life is like a sandwich! Birth as one slice, and death as the other. What you put in-between the slices is up to you. Is your sandwich tasty or sour?" —Allan Rufus

Currently, there are several conflicts globally due to religious, racial and regional intolerance. Embracing spiritualism is the only way to bring improvements in society. We brought nothing to this world when we were born. We will not carry anything from this world when we die except either a good or bad reputation. Hence, stress on spiritualism to spread peace and love in the world.

Life is an echo. If you do good things, you get back good things. Newton's third law of physics "For every action, there is an equal and opposite reaction" is applicable in this context. Hence, do good for others to build a better world. To conclude, spiritualism is the only way to provide meaning to your life and to build a better world.

"The more light you allow within you, the brighter the world you live in will be." —Shakti Gawain

References

Author's Vision 2030: https://professormsraovision2030.blogspot.com
Author's Amazon URL: http://www.amazon.com/M.-S.-Rao/e/B00MB63BKM
Author's LinkedIn: https://in.linkedin.com/in/professormsrao
Author's YouTube: http://www.youtube.com/user/profmsr7
Author's Facebook page: https://www.facebook.com/Professor-MS-Rao-451516514937414/
Author's Company Facebook Page: https://www.facebook.com/MSR-Leadership-Consultants-India-375224215917499/
Author's Instagram: https://www.instagram.com/professormsrao
Author's Blogs:
http://professormsraoguru.blogspot.com
http://professormsrao.blogspot.com
http://profmsr.blogspot.com
https://www.london.edu/faculty-and-research/lbsr/think-differently-rewire-your-brain#.WIyux1MrLIU
https://www.thriveglobal.com/stories/33909-lead-your-life-spiritually

2 – SEARCH MEANING FOR YOUR LIFE

"Those who have failed to work toward the truth have missed the purpose of living." —Buddha

Some people search meaning for their lives. They question themselves, "Who am I?", "What is my identity?", "Why did I come to this world?", "What is my role?" "What should be my goal?", "What I would like to be remembered for?" and so on. This inquiry spirit leads to individual growth and spiritual development. Some people go to the extent of giving up their materialistic possessions to search meaning for their lives. For instance, Buddha renounced all his materialistic possessions and luxuries to become a great saint.

From Siddhartha Gautama to Buddha (563-483 BC)

"Teach this triple truth to all: A generous heart, kind speech, and a life of service and compassion are the things which renew humanity." —Buddha

There are different versions of Buddha's reinvention from Siddhartha Gautama. Here is the most accurate one. Siddhartha Gautama was born to a Hindu King in Lumbini. He led a luxurious life since childhood. His father deliberately sheltered him from human sufferings particularly death. One day when he was passing through, he was shocked by the sight of an aged man, a sick man, and a corpse. He was deeply moved people crying over the dead body. These incidents made him think and find out who he was. He abandoned all comforts of the palace to seek enlightenment. He was enlightened at Bodh Gaya. He acquired the Three Knowledges[1]. The first knowledge was that of his past lives and the past lives of all beings. The second knowledge was of the laws of karma. The third knowledge was that he was free of all obstacles and released from attachments. During his enlightenment, Buddha discovered the following three great truths: nothing is lost in the universe; everything changes; and the law of cause and effect. He created the following 4 noble truths and the secret to true peace and happiness: The Noble Truth of Suffering; The Noble Truth of The Arising of Suffering; The Noble Truth of the Cessation of Suffering: Suffering Can Cease; and The Noble Truth of The Path leading to the Cessation of Suffering: There is a Path our of Suffering. He gave his first sermon in Sarnath. His wife Yasodhara became a nun and disciple his son, Rahula became a monk at the age of 7 and spent the rest of his life with his father. He spent many years teaching his philosophy of inner peace, detachment and how to attain liberation from earthly suffering. His doctrines eventually became what is known as Buddhism. He attained Mahaparinirvana in Kushinagar.

Who Am I?

"Who am I? Not the body, because it is decaying; not the mind, because the brain will decay with the body; not the personality, nor the emotions, for these also will vanish with death." —Ramana Maharshi

Ramana Maharishi made the question, 'Who Am I?' very popular. With the rapid growth in technologies, people are overloaded

---

1   https://www.thoughtco.com/the-enlightenment-of-the-bud-dha-449789

with information and lost track of their paths. They began questioning their nature of work and life. Hence, the question, 'who am I?' has become more popular currently. It is a well admitted fact that only when you love yourselves you will be able to love others. Only when you understand yourself you will be able to understand others. Hence, understand yourself through self-inquiry. The human mind is like a monkey's mind. When you can control and stabilize your mind, you will be able to inquire yourself to find meaning to your life.

Yevgeny Pushenko's Inspiring Spiritual Journey

MARC V. outlines an inspiring story of Yevgeny Pushenko who gave up everything to find meaning to his life in the article titled, '10 Refreshing Stories Of Rich People Who Gave Their Fortunes Away as follows: Yevgeny Pushenko[2] had a good thing going for him back in the 1990s. The Soviet Union had just broken up and people were free to pursue their dreams. For Pushenko, that freedom enabled him to construct a clothing factory in his hometown of Vladivostok. Soon, the business was booming and he had 50 factory workers at one point. However, Pushenko felt empty. Until then, he had not practiced his faith as an Orthodox Christian, which was suppressed for so long by the authorities. It wouldn't be long before he met his friends over vodka (of course) and handed them the keys to his factory. His shocked friends found out the reason from his parents the next day: He wanted to be a monk and do a pilgrimage to Jerusalem. For three years, Pushenko walked 15,000 kilometers (9,320 mi) through several countries until he finally reached his destination. Pushenko endured many trials during his journey, from battling extreme weather to fending off suspicious authorities, but remarked that his faith kept him going. After he had finished his pilgrimage, Pushenko renamed himself Athanassios and retired to Mt. Athos in Greece, where he has since resided at a monastery.

---

2 http://listverse.com/2013/12/24/10-refreshing-stories-rich-people-who-gave-their-fortunes-away/

Do Happiness and Meaning Go Together?

"Always remember that you are absolutely unique. Just like everyone else." —Margaret Mead

It is rare to achieve both happiness and meaning in life. The people who want to lead their lives happily are takers while the people who want to provide meaning to their lives are givers. When you lead a happy life, you live only one life. However, when you lead a meaningful life, you live beyond one life. Only in rare cases, you live in eternity. It all depends on the people and their choices whether they want to live for today or eternity. When you look at Mahatma Gandhi, Martin Luther King Jr, Mother Teresa and Nelson Mandela they sacrificed their personal lives for the sake of others by giving everything and provided meaning to their lives. You must strike a balance between happiness and meaning to lead a happy and meaningful life.

How to Lead a Meaningful Life?

"Identity is the role you chose to play in the story of the Universe." —Maria V Shall

To lead a purposeful life, break your mental limitations. Anthony Robbins said, "Many people are passionate, but because of their limiting beliefs about who they are and what they can do, they never take the actions that could make their dream a reality." Therefore, take risks. Remember, not to take a risk is also a risk. Identify your passions and follow them religiously. Remember, you have only one life to live. Focus on the destination but enjoy the journey. Remember, you must balance your personal, professional and social life. Above all, avoid regrets in life. To summarize, don't live your life on auto-pilot. Instead, take control; be a risk-taker; come out of your comfort zone; and explore opportunities to make it big in your life.

Conclusion

"Knowing others is wisdom, knowing yourself is enlightenment." —Lao Tzu

Thomas Jefferson[3] was the third president of the United States. In his final days, he insisted that his grave mention his status as founder of the University of Virginia; he did not want his tomb to mention that he was an American president. People are born and dead every day but we remember only a few great leaders because they added immense value to the society and provided meaning to their lives. Therefore, understand your identity to add value to others and provide meaning to your life.

"In the end these things matter most: How well did you love? How fully did you live? How deeply did you let go?" —Buddha

References

https://www.thoughtco.com/the-enlightenment-of-the-buddha-449789

https://www.monticello.org/site/research-and-collections/jeffersons-gravestone

http://listverse.com/2013/12/24/10-refreshing-stories-rich-people-who-gave-their-fortunes-away/

---

3   https://www.monticello.org/site/research-and-collections/jeffersons-gravestone

3 – Be a Mindful Leader to Lead Others Effectively

"No leader sets out to be a leader. People set out to live their lives, expressing themselves fully. When that expression is of value, they become leaders. So the point is not to become a leader. The point is to become yourself, to use yourself completely – all your skills, gifts and energies – in order to make your vision manifest. You must withhold nothing. You, must, in sum, become the person you started out to be, and to enjoy the process of becoming." —Warren Bennis, *On Becoming a Leader*

Most of the leadership literature revolves around leading others and deriving satisfaction from it. There is hardly any literature highlighting self-leadership currently. In fact, it is easy to preach to others to lead effectively. But what is most challenging is to convince yourself and lead yourself first to enable you to lead others. It is a well admitted fact that people can either preach or practice. But hardly there are people who can preach and practice. Most of the leadership literature is littered with many scholars, intellectuals and educators who do intensive research on leadership theories to create new models, styles, tools, and techniques. When they are asked to lead, they find it challenging to lead. At the same time, there are leaders who hit the ground by following the theory. They lead better than scholars, educators, intellectuals, and preachers. However, they cannot create new leadership theories and models due to a lack of theoretical mindset.

How to Lead Yourself First

"You can't lead people if you can't lead yourself. Self-leadership qualities qualifies you to become a co-operate leader." —Israelmore Ayivor, *Leaders' Ladder*

Here are some tools and techniques to lead yourself successfully.

- Analyze your strengths and weaknesses to enable you to capitalize your strengths and guard against your weaknesses.
- Identify your talents and skills. Build your skills around your talents. People waste their precious time by building talents around skills. Remember, leadership is more of a talent than a skill. Additionally, leadership is a blend of both nature and nurture. Some are partly acquired through heredity (nature) while the majority is acquired through learning, experience, and practice (nurture).
- Learn from the mistakes of others. It is rightly said that wise people learn from the mistakes of others while foolish people learn from their mistakes. Of course, we all become fools one day as we all make mistakes in our lives.
- Take calculated risks, and lead by trial and error. If you succeed, you become a leader; if you fail, you become a guide.
- Embrace failures but learn from them. Overcome the fear of failure that prevents people from leading.
- Inculcate a positive, right, and strong attitude. Don't let your failures distract your attention and disrupt your traction. Mac Anderson rightly remarked, "Great leadership usually starts with a willing heart, a positive attitude, and a desire to make a difference."
- Emphasize ideas rather than individuals. Avoid wasting your time on issues that disrupt your traction.

- Read books widely to understand various perspectives on leadership to put them into practice. President Truman rightly remarked, "Not all readers are leaders, but all leaders are readers." Remember, no amount of theoretical knowledge helps unless you put it into practice. You cannot become a crack shot unless you lose some ammunition. Be prepared to lose some energy, time, and resources while leading to achieve leadership effectiveness and excellence.
- Hire coaches or mentors to acquire leadership ideas and insights.
- Take feedback from reliable sources regularly to improve your leadership abilities and skills.
- Learn, unlearn and relearn because no specific styles and models work forever in leadership. Remember, leadership is a continuous learning process.
- Don't bother for criticism. Be thick-skinned to excel as a leader.

Become a Mindful Leader

"To handle yourself, use your head; to handle others, use your heart." —Eleanor Roosevelt

To grow as a mindful leader, you must pay more attention to what is happening "inside" than what is happening "outside." To become a mindful leader, regularly spend some to reflect your thoughts. Focus on your breath. Do meditation. Go for a mindfulness course or attend a workshop to understand mindfulness. Aldous Huxley remarked, "In all activities of life, the secret of efficiency lies in an ability to combine two seemingly incompatible states: a state of maximum activity and a state of maximum relaxation." Bill George[4] outlined six principle areas to lead yourself. They are gaining

4 http://www.billgeorge.org/page/true-north-discover-your-authentic-leadership

self-awareness; practicing your values and principles under pressure; balancing your extrinsic and intrinsic motivations; building your support team; staying grounded by integrating your life; and understanding your passion and purpose of your leadership.

Conclusion

> "Nothing so conclusively proves a man's ability to lead others as what he does from day to day to lead himself." —Thomas J. Watson, the former chairman of IBM

Leadership is easier said than done. John Maxwell quoted, "Leadership is more of a Crock-Pot proposition. It takes time, but the end product is worth the wait." Hence, come out of your comfort zone to evolve and excel as a leader. It is the unwise people who endeavor to conquer the world without conquering themselves. Peter F. Drucker rightly remarked, "You cannot manage other people unless you manage yourself first." Hence, conquer yourself to conquer others. Similarly, lead yourself first to lead others.

> "Go out and lead the world; but never forget to begin by leading yourself first at home. You can't lead the environment if you can't lead yourself in it." —Israelmore Ayivor, *Leaders' Watchwords*

References

http://www.billgeorge.org/page/true-north-discover-your-authentic-leadership

http://simplyg.com/lead-others-first-lead-john-c-maxwell/

4 – Excel as an Authentic Leader

"The thought of being a leader may seem like an appealing idea to the ego, but the reality of what being an authentic leader implies scares the ego to death. It means ego death. Why? Because it means that we actually care so much about a higher purpose, a higher principle, a higher goal, that we're willing to make the most important sacrifices for the sake of what we are aspiring to accomplish. It means we care so passionately about others also reaching that goal that we unhesitatingly sacrifice our own peace of mind, comfort, and security in order for them to succeed. It really means that we have no choice left anymore because we have realized without any doubt that from now on, it's up to us. We have realized that One Without a Second. We have realized that there is no other and there never could have been. What is so interesting about authentic leadership is this very insight: that once we have arrived, there is no longer any point of return. We have become one with destiny itself." —Andrew Cohen[5] on Authentic Leadership.

Leaders including Mahatma Gandhi, Martin Luther King Jr, Mother Teresa, Nelson Mandela, and Aung San Suu Kyi are

---

5   http://www.andrewcohen.org/andrew/authentic-leadership.asp

commonly connected through authentic leadership because they walked the talk and practiced what they preached. Similarly, corporate leaders including Bill Gates and Warren Buffett symbolize authentic leadership. They care for their stakeholders including employees, customers, shareholders, and society.

What is Authentic Leadership?

Avolio, Luthans, and Walumbwa[6] define authentic leaders as "those who are deeply aware of how they think and behave and are perceived by others as being aware of their own and others' values/moral perspectives, knowledge, and strengths; aware of the context in which they operate; and who are confident, hopeful, optimistic, resilient, and of high moral character." Authentic leadership is the ability to lead from the front with values and principles and through fairness, trust, and transparency. This leadership not only appears to be authentic at the surface level but also authentic at the core level. Truth, honesty, courage, convictions, and humility are the hallmarks of authentic leadership. It calls for complete synchronization between words and deeds.

Hallmarks of Authentic Leaders

Authentic leaders are different from others. They have a higher sense of self-awareness and have a more differentiated self-identity than other leaders. They exhibit a greater willingness and greater degrees of self-disclosure. They use ego or self-transcendental processes as exceptional responses to challenging circumstances. They are more likely to engage in self-sacrificing behaviors than others. They don't appeal to all as they are honest and straightforward. They mean business and don't appreciate manipulations. They are ready to break their relations to stick to their values and principles. Honesty and humility are the hallmarks of these authentic leaders. Here are some more hallmarks of authentic leaders. Authentic

---

6   http://www.samyoung.co.nz/2015/12/authentic-leaders-and-followers.html

leaders practice what they preach. They motivate and inspire others. They stand by with their team through thick and thin. They take total responsibilities and take on the battles relentlessly without any fear or favor. They take continuous feedback to improve themselves seriously. They are trendsetters rather than trend followers. They keep their people's interests above their personal interests. They create common cause through consensus. They believe in transparency. They roll up their sleeves wholeheartedly. They do what is right rather than what appears right. They strive for excellence, not perfection. They emphasize more on means than on ends.

Authenticity and humility are two sides of the same coin. Authentic leaders possess humility. Turnaround heroes are authentic leaders. Historically they demonstrated authentic leadership qualities by reviving their companies through sheer dint and hard work and through convictions and courage. Above all, authentic leaders are known for ethical values and principles. They don't believe in hype and appreciate doing things silently.

Excel as an Authentic Leader

"Leadership depends on an ability to call forth authentic action in response to the issues it identifies." —Bob Terry, *Authentic Leadership: Courage in Action*

Authentic leaders need to know about themselves to evolve and excel as authentic leaders. People love to be led by people without any positions and titles. Therefore, you should be ethical and transparent in all dealings unmindful of your leadership titles. You must stand by your convictions and set an example for others to emulate. You need to create goodwill and trust in your people. Additionally, it is essential to integrate authenticity in your leadership style to achieve an everlasting impact on the humankind. Above all, you need to accelerate your efforts and energies to excel as an authentic leader.

Spirituality and Authentic Leadership

"The authentic self is the soul made visible." —Sarah Ban Breathnach

Spirituality and authenticity are closely connected. Only when you are authentic you will be able to lead a spiritual life. Spiritual leaders leave their ego at the door. They are not narcissistic and arrogant. Humility and gratitude are the hallmarks of spiritual leaders. They emphasize values and morals, and principles and philosophies. In fact, ethics is an integral part of spiritual leadership and authentic leadership. When you want to lead spiritually, you must emphasize means, not ends to attain salvation.

Conclusion

"There could not be a better testing ground for leaders than the global economic meltdown. I believe all the economic misery, financial disasters and millions of lost jobs will produce a new generation of leaders who are battle-tested in crisis and ready to get the global economy pointed in a healthier long-term direction." —Bill George, *7 Lessons for Leading in Crisis*

Bill George[7] stated, "We need leaders who lead with purpose, values, and integrity; leaders who build enduring organizations, motivate their employees to provide superior customer service and create long-term value for shareholders." Hence, the world needs authentic leaders currently as the leadership and leaders are doubted due to the collapse of global companies including WorldCom, Enron, and Lehman Brothers. The criticism has gone to the extent of blaming business schools that are responsible for

---

7   http://citation.allacademic.com/meta/p_mla_apa_research_citation/1/3/7/9/4/pages137941/p137941-6.php

producing leaders without any emphasis on ethics and authenticity. To conclude, we must have authentic leaders who can bring forth courage and convictions, values and principles, fairness and transparency to take the humankind successfully to next higher orbit to leave a better legacy.

> "The credit belongs to the man who is actually in the arena, whose face is marred by dust and sweat and blood; who strives valiantly; who knows the great enthusiasm, the great devotions; who spends himself in a worthy cause; who at the best knows the triumph of high achievement and who if he fails, at least fails while daring greatly; so that his place shall never be with those cold and timid souls who neither know victory nor defeat." —Theodore Roosevelt

References

http://www.andrewcohen.org/andrew/authentic-leadership.asp

http://www.samyoung.co.nz/2015/12/authentic-leaders-and-followers.html

http://citation.allacademic.com/meta/p_mla_apa_research_citation/1/3/7/9/4/pages137941/p137941-6.php

Authentic Leadership: A Self, Leader, and Spiritual Identity Perspective by Karin Klenke International Journal of Leadership Studies, Vol. 3 Iss. 1, 2007, pp. 68-97

© 2007 School of Global Leadership & Entrepreneurship, Regent University ISSN 1554-3145

5 – Avoid Wearing Multiple Masks

"Virtue has a veil, vice a mask." —Victor Hugo

In this cut-throat competitive world, people wear different masks either to ensure their survival or to achieve success. Is it essential to wear them? What are the implications and complications involved in wearing multiple masks? Let us look at them.

Wearing a mask is to show something which you are not in reality. It is to fake to overcome your apprehensions or superstitions or weaknesses or anything which you want to hide them from others. Currently, people wear multiple masks. A few people are intelligent enough to identify such individuals behind their masks.

Some people wear multiple masks since they strive for validation and appreciation. You can fool some people for some time but you cannot fool all people all the time. Abraham Lincoln rightly remarked, "You may fool all the people some of the time, you can even fool some of the people all of the time, but you cannot fool all of the people all the time." When you look at social media people wear different masks, and it becomes nearly impossible to identify their real personalities.

Authors and story writers often wear multiple masks at the time of writing to enable them to get into the shoes of their characters to justify their content and get best out of it. It is like wearing multiples masks in an imaginary world.

Three Masks Most People Wear

"We all have a social mask, right? We put it on, we go out, put our best foot forward, our best image. But behind that social mask is a personal truth, what we really, really believe about who we are and what we're capable of." —Phil McGraw

People wear multiple masks in their personal, professional and social lives. In their personal life, they wear a mask to overcome their inner fears and phobias. In professional life, they wear a different mask to earn appreciation from their superiors and others. In social life, they show a different picture totally. It is like wearing multiple hats with multiple masks personally, professionally and socially.

Feel Good and Look Good

"The leader of men in warfare can show himself to his followers only through a mask, a mask that he must make for himself, but a mask made in such form as will mark him to men of his time and place as the leader they want and need." —John Keegan

People wear multiple masks due to various reasons. One of the reasons is the fear of rejection. They must understand that everyone has flaws. Most people understand this aspect, and hence, they accept and respect the flaws in others. It is a positive sign in the current world.

Some people believe that wearing multiple masks is not a bad idea as long as it serves their interests, and doesn't hurt or harm others. Some people go to the extent of justifying wearing multiple masks to achieve success by hook or crook.

People wear appealing clothes to please others. They demonstrate habits and practices to please others. They dress elegantly for events and functions to show to the people although they are not so in reality. It is to create 'feel good and look good' for them and others. When it is allowed, wearing multiple masks is also allowed to create feel good and look good around them.

There are no Ideal People in the World

"Behind every mask there is a face, and behind that a story." —Marty Rubin

Some people strive for perfection. If they cannot achieve it, they wear a mask. The reality is that there is nothing like perfection in this world. What we can do is to emphasize excellence. Secondly, there are no ideal people in the world as everyone has a hidden story behind them. Hence, it is ideal not to become idealistic but to strive for excellence irrespective of the area you belong to add value to you and the people around you.

It is rightly remarked that another person's pasture always looks greener. It is a well-admitted fact that nobody is perfect in the world. We are living in an imperfect world where people wear multiple masks from cradle to grave. Our imperfections make us unique and different from others.

You are a Gift to the World!

"I'm a very positive person, but this whole concept of having to always be nice, always smiling, always happy, that's not real. It was like I was wearing a mask. I was becoming this perfectly chiseled sculpture, and that was bad. That took a long time to understand." —Alicia Keys

Be what you are. Don't compare with others because you are a unique person and a gift to this world. You can take inspiration from other eminent leaders including Mahatma Gandhi, Mother Teresa, Nelson Mandela and Dalai Lama but you must not compare with them. The worst thing is to compare with others and wear masks accordingly. Additionally, don't sacrifice your personal happiness to please others because it is your life.

Unmask to Excel as an Authentic Leader

"We are what we pretend to be, so we must be careful about what we pretend to be." —Kurt Vonnegut

When you want to unlock your hidden potential, you must shed your mask. When you want to grow as a respectable leader, you must shed your mask. When you want to achieve success in the long-run, you must shed your mask. When you want to live beyond your lifetime, you must shed your mask. Mahatma Gandhi unveiled everything in his autobiographical book, *The Story of My Experiments with Truth.* Although people disliked some of his actions, they appreciated his principles of truth and non-violence. As a result, he lived beyond his lifetime. Hence, unmask to excel as an authentic leader.

Conclusion

"Wearing a mask wears you out. Faking it is fatiguing. The most exhausting activity is pretending to be what you know you aren't." —Rick Warren

When you wear a mask, you don't feel comfortable internally as your conscious repeatedly reminds your artificial face resulting in intrapersonal conflict. When you want to be loved for what you are, you must unmask yourself. Quetzal rightly remarked, "If you want people to love you for who you are, take the mask off."

We were born natural but we wear many masks during our lifetime. We wear multiple masks from cradle to grave due to innumerable reasons. But it is not advisable because everybody has their own flaws. Everybody has their strengths and weaknesses. Hence, there is no meaning in hiding them to please others. Remember, nobody is entirely good, and nobody is entirely bad. Every good leader has some flaws and every bad leader has some great things. To summarize, avoid wearing multiple masks. Instead, be authentic to keep yourself happy and excited. Have guts to face the realities in your life. Be what you are. Be natural. Be original. Be authentic to lead from your heart to stand out as a tall leader.

"The privilege of a lifetime is to become who you truly are." —C.G. Jung

6 – AVOID EXPLOITING OTHERS

"People were created to be loved. Things were created to be used. The reason why the world is in chaos is because things are being loved and people are being used." —Unknown

Several conflicts arise in society due to various reasons. One of the causes of conflict is when people exploit others' weaknesses instead of helping them. Some people take undue advantage out of others' adversities thus causing further hardships and agony. Although everyone knows that it is wrong to take advantage when others are in problems, people still resort to such activities. This chapter addresses the individuals who exploit others' weaknesses and offers a cautious message to the exploiters and manipulators.

Life is a Circus

"We live in a world where unfortunately the distinction between true and false appears to become increasingly blurred by manipulation of facts, by exploitation of uncritical minds, and by the pollution of the language." —Arne Tiselius

Life is a circus with ups and downs. We have friends and relatives to share our sorrows and happiness. What happens when one of your friends or relatives exploit your weaknesses when you are in deep distress. What happens when the person you trust lets you down? It is difficult to digest and cope up with the situation indeed!

It causes further stress and lands people in depression leading to suicides. Additionally, problems come in battalions. When your time is bad all problems come at a time. When you intend to handle one problem, other problems crop up simultaneously. In this scenario, instead of surrendering you must learn to fight against the odds. Remember the slogan 'when the going gets tough, tough gets going'. Hence, the best within you will come up when you are forced to the corner. You tend to think from multiple perspectives to overcome the challenges. You unlock your potential. Finally, the real leader within you emerges. Here are some tools to deal with being exploited by others:

- Don't trust others blindly.
- Don't reveal all your weaknesses to others.
- Don't get dejected.
- Be confident.
- Be mentally prepared to encounter unforeseen challenges.
- Be assertive. Raise your voice against irregularities.
- Don't indulge in self-blame and self-pity.
- Don't brood over the problems. Explore solutions to resolve them.

Remember, luck comes with interest while bad luck comes with a bonus. But don't lose your heart. Be brave to face the challenges squarely.

Caution to Exploiters and Manipulators

"I'm not upset that you lied to me, I'm upset that from now on I can't believe you." —Friedrich Nietzche

Don't be overambitious. Don't be an egotist. Don't be narcissistic. Don't be selfish. On the other hand, be compassionate. Don't be a "jerk" but be an "altruist." Be others-centered, not self-centered. Remember, neither success nor failure is permanent.

You may be in a strong position today but tomorrow you may be in a weak position. Remember, every dog has its own day. Hence, think of the pros and cons before exploiting others. Don't let the negative thoughts enter your mind. Fill your mind with positive thoughts to get energized.

At times, the exploiters and manipulators think that they are smart enough to cheat and exploit others. They must know the slogan, 'although the righteous man falls ten times, he rises, but the wicked man never falls twice'. If they still resort to exploitation and manipulation, it means their days are numbered.

Exploitation is Unavoidable

"Almost all of our relationships begin and most of them continue as forms of mutual exploitation, a mental or physical barter, to be terminated when one or both parties run out of goods." —W. H. Auden

Exploitation is everywhere in the world. As long as individuals with negative attitude live, the exploitation exists. Remember, exploitation is unavoidable. You must take your own precautions from exploiters and manipulators to lead a happy and exciting life.

Don't suffer silently with exploitation. Face with confidence. Fight for your rights. It is your life and you must make your call based on your convictions. Remember, there are no permanent friends and enemies in life. Life is all about rapid changing equations. Learn to face the challenges squarely. Fight to the finish. Take your battle to its logical end.

Conclusion

"Avoid those who seek friends in order to maintain a certain social status or to open doors they would not otherwise be able to approach." —Paulo Coelho, *Manuscript Found in Accra*

Empathy is key to resolving several conflicts globally. Being ambitious and confident are signs of good health but being over-ambitious and overconfident are signs of ill health. In fact, over-ambition and overconfidence are the worst enemies of individuals. Hence, people must understand the difference and adopt the right means and methods to gain acceptance in society to grow as healthy leaders. To conclude, it is not 'might is right' but 'right is right' is right.

"I call for a march from exploitation to education, from poverty to shared prosperity, a march from slavery to liberty, and a march from violence to peace." —Kailash Satyarthi

7 – Discipline Your Monkey Mind

"The mind is a wonderful servant, but a terrible master."
—Robin Sharma

The human mind is very powerful which can be used either for good or bad. Most people want to use it for doing constructive activities. However, it wanders and behaves like a monkey without any focus. At times, it leads to destructive activities causing damage to individuals and others. Why does it happen? Research shows that humans get around 60,000 thoughts in a day and mostly they are negative in nature. That is the reason why some people get into negative zone quickly ending up as failures. If humans know how to convert their negative thoughts into positive thoughts they will be able to live with peace and harmony and unlock their hidden potential. It is possible when they know how to control their monkey minds to consolidate their thoughts. In this context, let us discuss monkey mind, merits of taming it, and tips to discipline it to achieve your desired goals and objectives.

What is Monkey Mind?

"Distraction is the main problem for us all – what the Buddha called the monkey mind. We need to tame this monkey mind." —Tenzin Palmo

The monkey mind is a Buddhist term which is a state of undisciplined mind where it is chaotic and wanders without any self-control. The monkey mind is different from inner noise. The monkey mind is a chaotic mind and unstable mind whereas inner noise is a mental conversation causing irritation and leading to conflicts. It is often the monkey mind that leads to inner noise, not the other way around. Additionally, inner noise prevents smooth and successful communication. Monkey mind leads to confusion where individuals don't have clarity of what they are doing resulting in frequent failures and depression. Hence, it is essential to cure this mind by understanding it effectively. Here are some merits of disciplining your monkey mind. When you discipline your mind, you will be clear about goals and focus on them religiously. It enhances your concentration to do smart work instead of hard work. You achieve qualitative and multiple outcomes with a single effort. You sleep well and lead a happy and peaceful life.

Tips to Discipline Your Monkey Mind

"You can't stop the waves, but you can learn to surf." —Jon Kabat-Zinn

The monkey mind is unstable and erratic. It distracts the thought process and prevents ideas from popping up in your mind. It does not allow the scheduled activities to be executed effectively. Hence, it is essential to discipline it. At the same time, the monkey mind is a natural mental state for a moment, not a disease. But excessive monkey mind is a cause for concern. Here are some tips to discipline your monkey mind.

- Focus clearly on your goals. Set deadlines regularly to achieve one after another.
- Engage your mind productively on your passionate areas. Remember, an empty mind is like a devil's work. Pursue

your hobbies. Invest your time wisely on activities that help in your personal, professional and social life.

- Feed positive commands to your subconscious mind to make it stable to achieve all-round success.
- Convert your internal dialogue into a constructive and meaningful one.
- Change your food habits to tame your monkey mind. Eat a banana to improve your mood levels.
- Avoid skipping your breakfast. When you take breakfast, you can prevent blood-sugar fluctuations because blood-sugar fluctuations lead to poor focus as well as irritability and mood swings.
- Do meditation such as Yoga, Qigong, and Tai Chi regularly. Emphasize more on transcendental meditation (TM) and Qigong. Famous people including Oprah Winfrey, Ellen DeGeneres, Paul McCartney, and Beatle practice transcendental meditation. Qigong is a Chinese holistic wellness practice blending breathing and thinking. Dr. Mehmet Oz remarked, "If you want to be healthy and live to 100, do qigong."
- Do breathing exercises. Breathe in and hold for a few seconds and gradually breathe out. When more oxygen goes inside your brain, you will be able to quiet your mind and stabilize it. When you breathe in, focus your attention on the crown of your head and when you breathe out, you focus your attention on your navel. When you do so for a few times, you shift your attention from the crown of your head to your navel and discipline your monkey mind.
- Sleep well to relax your mind.
- Invest conscious efforts to quiet your monkey mind.

How do I Discipline my Monkey Mind?

Like other human beings, my mind also wanders. Being a creative author, my mind wanders frequently. Hence, I focus my mind on my creative activities such as writing. When I was unemployed in my life, instead of regretting lack of employment opportunities, I focused on sharing my knowledge free with the world to make a difference. I regularly woke up from my bed early morning with a goal to post articles on leadership, success, and spirituality. I wrote articles and blogged and shared them on social media platforms regularly. In this way, I engaged my mind constructively and shared my knowledge with the world free. It gave me a great sense of satisfaction and provided meaning to my life.

Whenever I wrote articles, many new ideas flashed in my mind simultaneously thus diverting my train of thoughts from writing. Hence, I stopped my writing for a moment and jotted down the ideas that popped up my mind and then I resumed my writing. In this way, I pleased my monkey mind, captured the ideas and continued to write with my flow of thoughts.

I started researching my passionate areas and authored over 45 books. In this way, I improved my writing skills and made a difference in the world. I did not earn any money but I received lots of appreciation mails from my followers globally. I felt excited to share more knowledge free with the people. When unemployed, most people are usually upset and depressed. But I converted the problem of unemployment into sharing knowledge free to build a better world. Remember, there are no problems but only prospects in life. It all depends on how you look at your life and the people around you. Hence, develop a positive, right and strong attitude toward life to engage your mind creatively and constructively to add value to the society and provide meaning to your life.

The human mind is unique and everyone has their own styles of taming their minds. Hence, people must customize solutions that suit their mindsets to discipline their minds to unlock their hidden potential.

Conclusion

"Learning to address concerns methodically, with reference to logic and empirical evidence, is one of the most useful things an anxious person can do." —Daniel B. Smith, *Monkey Mind: A Memoir of Anxiety*

Disputes arise in the workplace and within the family members due to the monkey mind. In fact, the monkey mind is responsible for most of the challenges in the world today. Hence, it is essential to discipline the monkey mind to build a healthy and peaceful world.

Everything is possible in this world when people develop a positive attitude and have willpower. Hence, believe in yourself and discipline your monkey mind to unlock your hidden potential to achieve success and make a difference in the lives of others. Controlling your monkey mind is the key to peace, happiness, and success. To conclude, acquire these tools and techniques to control your mind to unlock your potential to achieve all-round peace and prosperity in your life.

"Transcendental Meditation gives me an island of calm in the midst of so much turbulence." —Paul McCartney

8 – UNDERSTAND THE POWER OF YOUR SUBCONSCIOUS MIND

"The more intensely we feel about an idea or a goal, the more assuredly the idea, buried deep in our subconscious, will direct us along the path to its fulfillment." —Earl Nightingale

Your conscious and subconscious mind will bring many miracles in your life. If you understand and differentiate between them, you will be able to achieve amazing success in your life. Your conscious mind understands, reasons, and decides what information to accept and reject. In contrast, your subconscious mind doesn't have any reasoning. It doesn't argue, and it blindly follows what is fed by your conscious mind. People often talk about gut and intuition. In fact, they are closely connected with your subconscious mind. You can achieve anything and everything in your life if you build chemistry between your conscious and subconscious mind. Yvonne Oswald unveils in the book, *Every Word Has Power*[8], about the features of the subconscious as follows. The subconscious mind operates the physical body; has a direct connection with the Divine; remembers everything; stores emotions in the physical body; maintains genealogical instincts; creates and maintains least effort (repeating patterns); uses metaphor,

---

8 http://www.consciouslifestylemag.com/subconscious-mind-power/

imagery, and symbols; takes direction from the conscious mind; accepts information literally and personally; and does not process negative commands.

You can Accomplish Everything with Your Subconscious Mind

"The person with a fixed goal, a clear picture of his desire, or an ideal always before him, causes it, through repetition, to be buried deeply in his subconscious mind and is thus enabled, thanks to its generative and sustaining power, to realize his goal in a minimum of time and with a minimum of physical effort. Just pursue the thought unceasingly. Step by step you will achieve realization, for all your faculties and powers become directed to that end." —Claude M. Bristol

You can program your subconscious mind through your conscious mind. You can give instructions to accomplish your goals and objectives. Repeat your instructions to your subconscious mind to enable you to change your behavior. For instance, when you want to get employment with good pay and perks, you must give clear instructions to your subconscious mind repeatedly to enable you to be employed with a lucrative career. Similarly, when you want to find love, you can find it easily by giving instructions repeatedly to your mind accordingly. When you want to win a Nobel Prize, draw a long-term strategy and prepare your goals accordingly. Feed your subconscious mind repeatedly that you are winning the Nobel Prize. Earl Nightingale rightly remarked, "Whatever we plant in our subconscious mind and nourish with repetition and emotion will one day become a reality." Many analysts, thinkers, and researchers reveal that you can become the way you want to become. It is possible when you give your commands through your conscious mind to subconscious mind repeatedly. At the same time, you must work hard, smart and wise to accomplish your goals.

Improve Your Behavior to Excel as a Leader

"The truth is you can acquire any quality you want by acting as though you already have it." —Joseph Murphy

You can understand the subconscious mind of the people from their body language because the outward behavior of the people is nothing but the reflection of their subconscious mind. You can change the behavior of the people through the subconscious mind. Companies provide leadership development training to their employees to equip them with skills, abilities, and knowledge. At that time, the trainers must make use of the tools and techniques of the subconscious mind to improve the skills, abilities, and knowledge, and to change their behavior. Some people aspire to grow as leaders. Such people must understand the power of the subconscious mind and utilize it effectively to grow as leaders. Since leadership is a skill, not a talent, it is easy to change and improve behavior.

Let Go Off Your Unpleasant Past

"Busy your mind with the concepts of harmony, health, peace, and goodwill, and wonders will happen in your life." —Joseph Murphy

'Let go' is the philosophy to lead a happy, healthy, peaceful and successful life. Learn to forget and forgive others. Be compassionate. Avoid brooding over your unpleasant past. Forget unpleasant people and unpleasant experiences to lead a peaceful life. At the same time, don't allow the people who betrayed you in the past to avoid repeating the mistakes and regretting later.

A study shows that people waste most of their time by worrying about their unpleasant past that cannot be changed. Hence, don't worry about your unpleasant past and events. At the same time, don't excessively worry about the future that cannot be predicted. Learn to live in present with happiness and peace.

> "Whatever your conscious mind assumes and believes to be true, your subconscious mind will accept and bring to pass. Believe in good fortune, divine guidance, right action, and all the blessings of life." —Joseph Murphy

Reference

http://www.consciouslifestylemag.com/subconscious-mind-power/

9 – Heal Your Diseases and Illness with Your Subconscious Mind

"God is the source of my supply. His riches flow to me freely, copiously, and abundantly. All my financial and other needs are met at every moment of time and point of space; there is always a divine surplus." —Joseph Murphy

The mind is a state of thinking and it is a soft copy, unlike brain which is a hard copy. Everyone has one mind but it has two distinct functions such as conscious mind and subconscious mind. The conscious mind is objective, the waking mind and on the surface, while the subconscious mind is subjective, the sleeping mind and the deep self. Succinctly, a conscious mind can be compared with a commander while the subconscious mind with a follower. Joseph Murphy rightly remarked, "Your subconscious mind does not argue with you. It accepts what your conscious mind decrees. If you say, "I can't afford it," your subconscious mind works to make it true. Select a better thought. The decree, "I'll buy it. I accept it in my mind."" Whatever the commander orders the follower does it. That means whatever the conscious mind feeds to the subconscious mind, the latter does it automatically. However, subconscious mind corrects whenever the conscious mind wavers from main goals and objectives.

Conscious and Subconscious Mind—Examples and Illustrations

"It is only through your conscious mind that you can reach the subconscious. Your conscious mind is the porter at the door, the watchman at the gate. It is to the conscious mind that the subconscious looks for all its impressions." —Robert Collier

When you learn swimming initially, your conscious mind is active to understand the tricks of swimming. Once you learn the art of swimming, it is transferred to your subconscious mind. Similarly, when you learn driving newly, your conscious mind is active to acquire the tricks of it. Once you learn driving, it is transformed into your subconscious mind. That means whenever you learn anything new, your conscious mind is highly active and after mastering, it is shifted to your subconscious mind to take of care it. While driving some people talk to their cell phones because they drive the car from their subconscious mind and speak through the phone from their conscious mind. That is the power of the subconscious mind!

Accomplish Your Goals through Your Subconscious Mind

"Write your goals down in detail and read your list of goals every day. Some goals may entail a list of shorter goals. Losing a lot of weight, for example, should include mini-goals, such as 10-pound milestones. This will keep your subconscious mind focused on what you want step by step." —Jack Canfield

Your conscious mind clicks off once you go to sleep while your subconscious mind is always attentive and never sleeps. That means your subconscious mind works both during waking and sleeping hours. It works round the clock without any rest. Hence, you must know how to give positive and healthy instructions to your subconscious mind to accomplish whatever you want. For instance, you can pass on your goals to your subconscious mind through repetition and it checks your conscious mind whenever the conscious mind deviates from your goals.

Heal Your Diseases and Illness

"The first thing to remember is the dual nature of your mind. The subconscious mind is constantly amenable to the power of suggestion; furthermore, the subconscious mind has complete control of the functions, conditions, and sensations of your body. Trust the subconscious mind to heal you. It made your body, and it knows all of its processes and functions. It knows much more than your conscious mind about healing and restoring you to perfect balance." —Joseph Murphy

There are several advantages to your subconscious mind. When you want to heal any disease or illness, you can easily heal them. When you give clear and constructive instructions to your subconscious mind you can cure your disease or illness. There are cases where cancer patients survived due to their will power. There are cases where people overcame their illness without any medication. They are possible when you know how you can give clear and constructive instructions to your subconscious mind. For instance, when people suffer from cancer, they must instruct their subconscious mind 5 or 10 minutes going to sleep as follows: "My cancer is curable and I am overcoming from my cancer." When someone has back pain, he or she must give instructions to the subconscious mind as follows: "My back pain is easily curable. I am perfectly comfortable without back pain. I can walk well with comfort. I am able to lift weights without any pain." In this way, people suffering from diseases and illness must give instructions to their subconscious mind before going to sleep by customizing as per their requirements. They will be able to overcome their diseases, illness, and challenges successfully. A study shows that when we go to sleep our conscious mind clicks off and our subconscious mind clicks on, and begins to entertain itself during the rest of the sleep. What we did in our last 30 minutes we replay 15-17 times during the night.

Disease versus Illness

There is a difference between disease and illness. Disease can affect an organ or organism, and illness is the result of it. At times disease can occur to mind leading to illness. Illness is not feeling well. It is a kind of discomfort and tiredness. It is mostly the outcome of the disease. In 1978, Eric Cassell[9] established the distinction between disease and illness by saying "disease ... is something an organ has; illness is something a man has." Both disease and illness are different. In fact, both are undesirable and indicate the symptoms of an abnormality in the system. In most cases, illness can be cured while in some cases diseases cannot be cured.

Give instructions from your conscious mind to your subconscious mind repeatedly that you will cure your diseases and overcome your illness. When you do so repeatedly, you will be able to heal yourself. Remember, you cannot live beyond your fixed lifespan by following it but you can live healthy, happily and peacefully.

Templates to be Happy and Healthy

"Never finish a negative statement; reverse it immediately, and wonders will happen in your life." —Joseph Murphy

Here are some messages you can give to your subconscious mind repeatedly: I am hale and hearty. I have control over my disease and illness. I can overcome them easily because they are only temporary. I get good from others because I do good to others.

---

9   https://www.reference.com/health/difference-between-disease-illness-b69e4a32392e4c5f

My biggest strengths are forgiveness and gratitude. I can overcome the disease and illness since I forgive others easily and forget the unpleasant events quickly. I was born to live a long and happy life. I was born to make a difference in society. Hence, I live longer to add value to society.

Conclusion

"Every thought is a cause & every condition is an effect. Change your thoughts & you change your destiny." —Joseph Murphy

Understand the power of your subconscious mind to heal diseases and illness without any medication to keep you healthy and happy. Joseph Murphy remarked, "Forgive yourself and everyone else before you go to sleep, and healing will take place much more rapidly."

"For those who believe, no proof is necessary. For those who don't believe, no proof is possible." —Stuart Chase

References

https://www.reference.com/health/difference-between-disease-illness-b69e4a32392e4c5f

http://www.amazon.in/Power-your-Subconscious-Mind/dp/1416511563

The Power of your Subconscious Mind by Dr. Joseph Murphy Revised by Dr. Ian McMahan (Simon & Schuster; Re-issue edition, 3 January 2006)

10 – Control Your Anger by Forgiving Others

"Holding on to anger is like grasping a hot coal with the intent of throwing it at someone else; you are the one who gets burned." —Buddha

Everyone gets angry in life. Some people get angry often while some people get angry seldom based on their emotions, mindset, and personality. In fact, anger is unavoidable in life. It is easy to control anger if people understand about themselves, and the people around them. Anger is the worst enemy in life that destroys relations forever and brings ill will among the people. Some people find it tough to conquer anger. In fact, anger is associated with emotions and can be managed easily by adopting certain tools and techniques. Some of the tools include wedding to spiritualism and doing meditation.

Anger Management

"Anger is an acid that can do more harm to the vessel in which it is stored than to anything on which it is poured." — Mark Twain

Anger is very harmful to the human body and mind. People lose sleep and develop anxiety. It has adverse effects on others. People forget what they do during anger because they often lose their mental balance. Anger is often dangerous leading to misunderstanding, violence, and crimes. Hence, people must identify the reasons for their anger and address them earnestly and immediately to contain further damage and loss. However, there are people who converted their anger into aggression to unlock their hidden potential to excel as extraordinary achievers. Wayne Dyer rightly remarked, "There's nothing wrong with anger provided you use it constructively." Therefore, it all depends on people how they address anger and channel it effectively.

Anger is a Double-Edged Sword

"There are two things a person should never be angry at, what they can help, and what they cannot." —Plato

If you channel anger constructively, you can achieve miracles in your life. In contrast, if you use it destructively, you ruin your prospects and peace in life. When anger goes out of control, it plays havoc. It damages personal, professional and social relations, and lowers prestige and image. There are ample examples where years of relationship and friendship is lost because of anger. Hence, it is essential to control your anger to lead a happy, peaceful and pleasant life.

Tools and Techniques to Tame Your Anger

"Bitterness is like cancer. It eats upon the host. But anger is like fire. It burns it all clean." —Maya Angelou

Here are some tools and techniques to control your anger.

- Be calm before you comment. Speak assertively. Remember, neither aggressiveness nor submissiveness works in this world. What works is assertiveness. To speak assertively, you must remain cool, calm and composed. Don't attack the individuals but attack only issues to resolve them amicably.

- Analyze the root causes and address them earnestly. Socrates rightly remarked, "An unexamined life is not worth living."
- Separate your emotions from issues and explore ideas to resolve the issues. Don't look at *who* is right and wrong but look at *what* is right and wrong. William Arthur Ward remarked, "It is wise to direct your anger towards problems — not people; to focus your energies on answers — not excuses."
- Count numbers from one to ten and in the reverse order to divert your attention from anger. Mark Twain remarked, "When angry, count four. When very angry, swear."
- Write the issues that create anger in your mind on paper and burn it. It decreases your anger to a great extent.
- Avoid making hasty decisions when in anger. Postpone the devil of decision-making. Ensure that your head rules over your heart.
- Go for a walk before making a decision. It energizes your body and helps you think analytically and logically.
- Doing exercises regularly enable the endorphins to calm you down and serve as an outlet for your rage. Here are some physical activities such as running, cycling, swimming, boxing, and dancing help you control your anger.
- Breathe deeply in through your nose and exhale through your mouth to help your body relax. It helps more oxygen go inside your brain thus relieving your tension and anger.
- Drink water to cool down yourself.
- Emphasize excellence, not perfection. You may get upset when you stress on perfection.
- Develop flexibility and adaptability. Don't try to change everything around you. There are certain things that are beyond human control. Understand this reality to eliminate your anger.
- Take breaks periodically to overcome stress and unwind yourself.

- Don't be oversensitive to the issues. Focus on bigger issues and offer your ideas. In this way, you forget your anger and focus on solutions rather than the problems. Precisely, become part of the solution, not the problem.
- Don't expect anything from others. Empathize and understand their limitations.
- Avoid perceptions. We often look at the world the way we are, not the way they are. Look at the issues with new lenses.
- Avoid focusing on stressful people, and unpleasant events and experiences. Let go off the past. Thich Nhat Hanh said, "Letting go gives us freedom, and freedom is the only condition for happiness. If, in our heart, we still cling to anything – anger, anxiety, or possessions – we cannot be free."
- Forgive the people who let you down to eliminate anger forever. Forgiveness is the greatest trait in human beings. Cherie Carter-Scott rightly remarked, "Anger makes you smaller, while forgiveness forces you to grow beyond what you are."

I served in the Indian Air Force, and I was very aggressive in my younger days. I have made a few mistakes due to my anger. Now I realize that I was wrong. I also began forgiving people especially my relatives who cheated me and put me into lots of problems financially. It gave me a great sense of satisfaction and happiness. Whenever I see people getting angry on trivial issues and on others I smile at them. I enjoy recalling what Thich Nhat Hanh quoted: "I would not look upon anger as something foreign to me that I have to fight... I have to deal with my anger with care, with love, with tenderness, with nonviolence."

Conclusion

"Anger and intolerance are the enemies of correct understanding." —Mahatma Gandhi

Remember, there are no permanent friends and foes in life. At times, it is the perceptions or egos that lead to anger and conflicts. Hence, adopt the tools and techniques to tame your anger to lead a happy and peaceful life.

"If we really want to love, we must learn how to forgive." — Mother Teresa

11 – FIGHT AGAINST FATIGUE

"Addiction, self-sabotage, procrastination, laziness, rage, chronic fatigue, and depression are all ways that we withhold our full participation in the program of life we are offered. When the conscious mind cannot find a reason to say no, the unconscious says no in its own way." —Charles Eisenstein

In this cut-throat competitive and complex world, people often fatigue a lot and fight against fatigue. The people who follow work-life balance to provide meaning to their lives keep fatigue at a bay. In this chapter, we will discuss fatigue and its causes, effects, and remedies.

Fatigue is about tiredness arising out of stress and burnout. When people work excessively beyond the capacity of their brain and body without giving adequate rest, they get fatigue. Fatigue[10] is defined as the temporary inability, or decrease in ability, or strong disinclination to respond to a situation, because of the previous over-activity, either mental, emotional or physical. Tom Cunningham remarked, "Fatigue is a state of mind. If you are very tired and then, suddenly, one minute later you find out you won a BIG lottery, your tiredness would vanish immediately. Why? Because your thoughts are excited about the future and its many

---

10 http://www.worksafe.govt.nz/worksafe/information-guidance/all-guidance-items/stress-and-fatigue-their-impact-on-health-and-safety-in-the-workplace/stress.pdf

possibilities. What changed from one minute ago? You don't even actually possess the money at that point and yet you are full of energy and likely won't sleep for many hours."

Types of Fatigue

"Massage therapy has been shown to relieve depression, especially in people who have chronic fatigue syndrome; other studies also suggest benefit for other populations." — Andrew Weil

Fatigue can be either acute or chronic. Acute fatigue is for short periods while chronic fatigue is for long periods. Acute fatigue is due to overdoing of tasks without giving adequate rest while chronic fatigue is due to the prolonged nature of mental and physical tasks without caring for body and brain. Acute fatigue can be handled easily while chronic fatigue can be handled by experts and professionals.

Causes and Effects of Fatigue

"The formula was simple: $E + F + C = M$. That is, excitement plus fatigue, plus confusion equals mistakes." —Rutledge Etheridge, *Agent of Destruction*

There are innumerable causes of fatigue. When people sit continuously for hours in front of the TV or computer screen they develop fatigue. The other reasons include being a couch potato, maintaining bad posture, lack of physical activities, and undisciplined eating.

The adverse effects of fatigue include lack of concentration and focus on the tasks, sluggish thinking, inability to perform physical and mental tasks, mood swings, forgetfulness, poor communication and decision-making, confusion, and lethargy. Fatigue leads to loss of memory, inability to recall information, increased accidents, and reduced productivity and performance in the workplace. Other challenges include anxiety, depression, sleep disorders, weight loss, muscle weakness, and cardiac-related problems to name a few.

Tools and Techniques to Fight against Fatigue

"A positive mental attitude will create more miracles than any wonder drug." —Patricia Neal

Here are some tools and techniques to fight against fatigue.

- Improve your lifestyle and attitude toward life.
- Bond with your family because family gives you emotional strength, happiness, and joy.
- Ensure a steady flow of income to avoid financial difficulties.
- Boost your brain and body by taking a perfect breakfast.
- Avoid taking large meals. Instead, take meals often in little quantity.
- Exercise regularly. Kerry J Stewart remarked, "Exercise has consistently been linked to improved vigor and overall quality of life. People who become active have a greater sense of self-confidence."
- Lose excess weight. Ensure that you maintain weight as per your sex, age, and height.
- Drink moderately. Avoid excessive alcohol that depresses the central nervous system.
- Have sex regularly. Sex releases stress, boosts your immunity power and brings happiness and joy.
- Pursue hobbies to unlock your potential and creativity.
- Take breaks periodically to recharge yourself. Travel to unwind yourself.
- Don't get addicted to technology especially social media. Use it judiciously.
- Emphasize physical interaction over virtual interaction.

- Join nonprofits to serve society. It keeps you away from fatigue apart from providing meaning to your life.
- Learn to be happy with what you have rather than worrying about others' prosperity. Remember, another person's pasture always looks greener. You don't know the real challenges being encountered by others who appear to be prosperous and happy externally.

In a nutshell, eat the right food at regular intervals. Identify any food allergies to avoid them. Hydrate your body by drinking lots of water. Walk regularly to energize your body. Do meditation. Get some Omega-3. Sleep well to recharge yourself. Consult doctor, if you get fatigue frequently.

Emphasize Work-Life Balance

"Just living is not enough ... one must have sunshine, freedom, and a little flower." —Hans Christian Andersen

The drivers who drive for long distance often get fatigue leading to accidents. The manual workers who work for long hours often get fatigue leading to workplace challenges. The researchers who do intensive research often get fatigue. It is obvious that anything that is excessively done without giving adequate break results in fatigue. Workaholism is mostly a bane than a boon. Although it gives you temporary results, the long-term repercussions are disastrous. Hence, it is essential to balance personal, professional and social life to lead a meaningful life.

Conclusion

"I had learned quickly that life doesn't always go the way I want it to, and that's okay. I still plod on." —Sarah Todd Hammer, *Determination*

Fatigue is an outcome of doing tasks excessively without giving the needed break affecting both brain and body. Hence, stay away from stress by ensuring work-life balance. If fatigue is recurrent, address it earnestly and effectively by doing activities that bring happiness and joy. Your life is in your hands. You must know how to lead your life happily and successfully. To conclude, lead your life with happiness and joy by staying away from fatigue.

"Life can make a person weary and wary, and the body and soul become fatigued. Unalleviated tedium extinguishes the light in the soul." —Kilroy J. Oldster, *Dead Toad Scrolls*

Reference

http://www.worksafe.govt.nz/worksafe/information-guidance/all-guidance-items/stress-and-fatigue-their-impact-on-health-and-safety-in-the-workplace/stress.pdf

12 – Overcome Your Depression

"Depression has been called the world's number one public health problem. In fact, depression is so widespread it is considered the common cold of psychiatric disturbances. But there is a grim difference between depression and a cold. Depression can kill you." —David D. Burns

Do you have knots in your stomach? Do you feel the sinking of your heart? Do you get negative thoughts in your mind frequently? Do you get suicidal tendencies? Then you are under depression. Depression is a major challenge globally leading to deaths and suicides. People are unable to cope up with it and express it with others when they are under depression. Even the eminent celebrities have depression leading to suicides. The World Health Organization[11] characterizes depression as one of the most disabling disorders in the world, affecting roughly one in five women and one in ten men at some point in their lifetime. It is estimated that 21% of women and 12% of men in the U.S will experience an episode of depression at some point in their lifetime.

What is Depression?

"Do not brood over your past mistakes and failures as this will only fill your mind with grief, regret and depression. Do not repeat them in the future." —Swami Sivananda

---

11 http://mentalhealth.fitness/learn-about-your-diagnosis/depression/

Depression is a state of mind. It is a momentary mental disorder. It involves negative self-talk thus draining energy and enthusiasm. There is a difference between sadness and depression. Sadness is for a short period while depression is for a long period. Sadness is a momentary feeling while depression is a negative feeling which is recurrent and sometimes beyond human control. Hence, depression can be defined as an extension of sadness. It is an unchecked stage of sadness where people recurrently think about their unpleasant past or experiences. Rollo May remarked, "Depression is the inability to construct a future." Barbara Kingsolver remarked, "There is no point treating a depressed person as though she were just feeling sad, saying, 'There now, hang on, you'll get over it.' Sadness is more or less like a head cold; with patience, it passes. Depression is like cancer." Here are some symptoms of depression: feeling worthlessness and helpless; doubting abilities, decreased energy levels, loss of interest in work, feeling irritation and isolation; eating disorders and sleeping disorders to name a few.

Causes of Depression

"If you don't think your anxiety, depression, sadness and stress impact your physical health, think again. All of these emotions trigger chemical reactions in your body, which can lead to inflammation and a weakened immune system. Learn how to cope, sweet friend. There will always be dark days." —Kris Carr

Depression is adversely affecting millions of people globally. Most people don't disclose for fear of losing their social status or ostracized by society. They hesitate to unveil as people might be excessively sympathetic to them which is not appreciated by them. As a result, they suffer from depression silently. There are innumerable causes of depression. Here are some of them. Volatility, uncertainty, complexity, and ambiguity (VUCA) is one of the major causes. Most people are comfortable with certainty.

Hence, they remain in their comfort zone which doesn't lead to human growth. When people are ambitious to grow, they encounter lots of challenges. They find it difficult to manage leading to depression. Rapid growth in technologies is another reason responsible for depression. People have become slaves to technology. They don't use it judiciously. When people compare with extraordinary achievers, they get into depression for their inability to grow. They hardly realize how much the extraordinary achievers have endured to come up to such level. It is also due to genetic reasons where the person gets depressed due to family history.

Technology and Depression

"Human bodies are designed for regular physical activity. The sedentary nature of much of modern life probably plays a significant role in the epidemic incidence of depression today. Many studies show that depressed patients who stick to a regimen of aerobic exercise improve as much as those treated with medication." —Andrew Weil

Technology is more of a bane than a boon to the people because it led to several health complications including depression. We cannot afford to stay away from technology altogether because technology has connected with the globe and converted into a small village, and improved the quality of human lives. We must draw a line clearly how to use technology wisely for the benefit of humankind. Excessive use of the internet, smartphones, and gadgets have made things worse for human beings leading to health hazards.

How to Overcome Your Depression?

"You largely constructed your depression. It wasn't given to you. Therefore, you can deconstruct it." —Albert Ellis

There is nothing wrong with depression but failing to identify and take appropriate timely measures is wrong. Depression is a state of mind where people are confused with negative or unpleasant thoughts. If they take remedial action timely by converting their negative thoughts into positive thoughts they will be able to overcome depression. Here are some ways to overcome depression:

- Be confident and optimist. Faith is the force of life. Hence, have faith in yourself.
- Don't be oversensitive to problems because problems are part of life.
- Don't feel shy to express your depression with others. Talk to friends and relatives to express your inner emotions and feelings.
- Don't get into a vicious circle. Instead, associate with positive people. A person is judged by the way he or she makes friends and wears clothes. Hence, choose healthy friends and wear comfortable clothes to create positive vibes.
- Do things that make you upbeat and energetic.
- Set your goals and focus on them religiously. Break them into long-term and short-term goals. And break short-term goals further into daily goals and work on them regularly. It helps you stay focused on your goals thus avoiding depression.
- Spend some time with nature. Richard Louv remarked, "Time spent in nature is the most cost-effective and powerful way to counteract the burnout and sort of depression that we feel when we sit in front of a computer all day."
- Pursue creative hobbies.
- Prefer physical interaction to virtual interaction.
- Participate in social activities and group activities. Contribute through nonprofits to serve society during your leisure time. It gives you immense satisfaction and meaning to your life.
- Do meditation regularly to control your emotions and thoughts. Meditation controls your emotions and stabilizes your mind.

- Eat the right food containing omega 3 fatty acids to get positive moods. Take Omega-3s through walnuts, flaxseed and oily fish like salmon or tuna to lower cholesterol and improve cardiovascular health. If required, consult a professional nutritionist.
- Avoid alcohol and caffeine.
- Do breathing exercises every day. When you inhale and exhale deeply more oxygen goes to your mind thus relieving your tension and anxiety.
- Exposé yourself to sunlight every day for some time. It gives you vitamin D and strengthens your bones.
- Give adequate rest to your mind by sleeping.
- Use technology judiciously. These days technology is essential to update and upgrade yourself. But don't get addicted to technology. Make it as your servant but don't become a servant to it.
- Don't worry about failures as they are the steppingstones to your next success. And don't worry about the results as long as you have contributed your best. Mother Teresa once remarked, "Do not allow yourselves to be disheartened by any failure as long as you have done your best."
- Don't compare with other achievers. For some people, success comes early and for some people, success comes late. Success is sure to come when you work hard and put your efforts relentlessly. You are a unique person and God's gift to this world. Hence, don't compare with others.
- Develop a positive attitude toward facing challenges. Accept the fact that there are many things that are beyond human control. Hence, there is no point in being overly concerned about the factors that cannot be controlled. Accept the fact that everything takes its own time to resolve. Only when the time comes, certain problems can be resolved. Until then, focus on your productive and creative activities.
- Develop the attitude of gratitude. Thank the people who helped you and laid the ladder for your success.

- Have a big heart to forgive others. Revenge ruins your life while forgiveness elevates your moods in life and makes you taller in the world.
- Avoid workaholism and wed spiritualism.
- Ensure work-life balance.
- Follow the philosophy of health first, education second, and wealth third.
- Consult a professional mental health practitioner, if you think that it is difficult for you to handle, and if you get suicidal tendencies frequently.

The strong family connection is the key to the success of great people. The family stands by you during your trials and tribulations by giving you emotional support. Technology cannot replace the power of family relations. Technology gives you a temporary excitement but your family gives you permanent peace and happiness. Additionally, an empty mind is like a devil's workshop. Hence, engage your mind productively on your passionate tasks. It helps you overcome depression and gives you productive results.

Depressed people need a shoulder to cry on. If you come across someone who is depressed, spend some time with them. Lend your ears. Use humor carefully. Grenville Kleiser remarked, "Good humor is a tonic for mind and body. It is the best antidote for anxiety and depression. It is a business asset. It attracts and keeps friends. It lightens human burdens. It is the direct route to serenity and contentment." Do the best you can timely to help the person overcome depression.

Conclusion

"Through my own struggles with depression, I discovered that knowledge, therapy, medication and education can provide the strength to get through it in one piece." —Susan Polis Schutz

Life is full of highs and lows. Every fall has a rise and every rise has a fall. Understand this fact and lead a balanced life. Don't get dejected by failures and don't get overjoyed by successes. Handle depression with a cool, calm and composed mind. To summarize, depression is a curable temporary mental disorder. You can overcome it easily by identifying and taking appropriate timely remedial measures. To conclude, improve your attitude toward your life to overcome depression to lead a happy and pleasant life.

"Our Generation has had no Great war, no Great Depression. Our war is spiritual. Our depression is our lives." —Chuck Palahniuk, Fight Club

Reference

http://mentalhealth.fitness/learn-about-your-diagnosis/ depression/

13 – Stay Younger and Live Longer

"Age is an issue of mind over matter. If you don't mind, it doesn't matter." —Mark Twain

Most people want to stay younger and live longer but only a few succeed. Everybody is not gifted to live longer. However, everyone can endeavor to stay younger and happier. It is essential to have a positive mindset, the right attitude and adopt healthy habits and practices to stay younger and live longer.

As you age, your body changes but your subconscious mind never grows old. Your character, convictions, mind, and faith are not subject to decay. Joseph Murphy remarked, "You grow old when you lose interest in life when you cease to dream, to hunger after new truths, and to search for new worlds to conquer. When your mind is open to new ideas and new interests and when you raise the curtain and let in the sunshine and inspiration of new truths of life and the universe, you will be young and vital." He further added, "A person's body slows down gradually as he or she advances through the years, but his conscious mind can be made much more active, alert, alive, and quickened by the inspiration from his or her subconscious mind."

How to Stay Younger and Live Longer?

"There are many tired gardeners but I've seldom met old gardeners. I know many elderly gardeners but the majority are young at heart. Gardening simply does not allow one to be mentally old, because too many hopes and dreams are yet to be realized. The one absolute of gardeners is faith. Regardless of how bad past gardens have been, every gardener believes that next year will be better. It is easy to age when there is nothing to believe in, nothing to hope for, gardeners, however, simply refuse to grow up." —Allan Armitage

When you want to stay younger and happier, you must love others and learn continuously because as long as you love and learn, you are young and the day you stop loving and learning, you become old. Henry Ford rightly remarked, "Anyone who stops learning is old, whether at twenty or eighty. Anyone who keeps learning stays young. The greatest thing in life is to keep your mind young." Dream big to achieve big. Dreams raise your hopes to accomplish new things thus enhancing your longevity and providing meaning to your life. C.S. Lewis quoted, "You are never too old to set another goal or to dream a new dream." Associate with healthy and positive people to enable you to spend your time and life positively. Here are some steps to keep younger and happier forever. Take healthy food to keep your body and mind healthy. Do physical exercises regularly. Have sex regularly. Mehmet Oz, MD, professor of surgery and vice-chairman of cardiovascular services at New York-Presbyterian/Columbia University rightly remarked, "Loving touches release hormones, including oxytocin that reduces stress and anxiety." Face challenges squarely. Love yourself to love others. Protect yourself to protect others.

- Pursue creative hobbies. Louise Nevelson quoted, "I never feel age … If you have creative work, you don't have age or time." Go for gardening to unwind yourself.
- Take little food but more times in a day. Usually, people take food three times but it is advisable to take food 5 or 6 times in small portions. To avoid overeating, drink a glass of water before taking food.
- Feel young at heart and sleep well. The human body needs 6 to 8 hours of sleep. Adequate sleep increases your energy

levels as you give rest to your body. It also increases your immunity. Dr. Jennifer Landa, MD, Chief Medical Officer of BodyLogicMD and author of The Sex Drive Solution for Women says, "Without high quality and quantity of sleep, your metabolism can slow to a crawl. It can also increase storage of deadly visceral fat around your organs."

- Emphasize physical relations over digital relations.
- Develop a sense of humor. Learn to laugh as laughter is great medicine for both the body and the mind.
- Exercise regularly because it has a tremendous impact on the brain. It helps prevent memory loss, cognitive decline, and dementia.
- Combat stress because stress makes you older mentally.
- Travel to different places to see various kinds of people and enjoy nature. It rejuvenates and makes you younger.
- Avoid alcohol. If at all you want to consume, drink moderately.
- Embrace change effectively. Accept the fact that only thing constant in the world is change. Charles Darwin remarked, "It is not the strongest of the species that survives, nor the most intelligent that survives. It is the one that is the most adaptable to change." Hence, adapt yourself.
- Spend your time with children as they are innocent and playful. Children bring you joy and happiness. They connect you with your past. They remind your childhood days.

I always feel young at heart as I associate with students regularly. Students are energetic and young in thoughts, ideas, and approaches. They add a new dimension to your thoughts and constantly keep you younger.

Follow Healthy Food Habits

"The secret of staying young is to live honestly, eat slowly, and lie about your age." —Lucille Ball

You must change your lifestyle and food habits to live longer and happier. If you are disciplined in your daily life, you can stay younger and live longer happily. Here are some foods to consider staying younger and living longer happily—oysters, green tea, grapes, shiitake mushrooms, clams, detox water, grapefruit, cooked sardines, walnuts, blueberries, rooibos tea, whole grain bread, spinach and banana smoothies, spinach, baked sweet potato, cherry tomatoes, yogurt, carrot, pomegranate, apples, raw salmon, tart cherries, milk, blackberries, and kale. Noshing on leafy vegetables like kale, collards and mustard greens that contain high vitamin K content can help slow cognitive decline, according to new research[12] that reviewed the diets of nearly 1,000 participants. In fact, the researchers discovered that people who ate one to two servings of the greens daily had the cognitive ability of a person 11 years younger than those who consumed none.

Conclusion

"I believe it's important to stay young at heart, to have faith in what might seem impossible and to have goals beyond your current abilities or temporary means." —Hayley Williams

To summarize, think good and do good. Allow positive thoughts and inspire others with your positive and appreciative words because what goes around comes around. Love the people around. Learn to be happy because happiness is in your hands. Laugh at yourself. To conclude, follow the right habits and practices to stay younger and live longer to enjoy your life. Frank Lloyd Wright quoted, "The longer I live the more beautiful life becomes." Life is beautiful!

"There is a fountain of youth: it is your mind, your talents, the creativity you bring to your life and the lives of people

---

12 http://www.bestlifeonline.com/foods-to-keep-you-young-forever

you love. When you learn to tap this source, you will truly have defeated age." —Sophia Loren

References

http://www.bestlifeonline.com/foods-to-keep-you-young-forever

http://www.shape.com/lifestyle/beauty-style/forever-young-5-ways-beat-clock-life

The Power of your Subconscious Mind by Dr. Joseph Murphy Revised by Dr. Ian McMahan (Simon & Schuster; Re-issue edition, 3 January 2006)

14 – Be a Pioneer of the Future, not a Prisoner of the Past

"Every time you are tempted to react in the same old way, ask yourself if you want to be a prisoner of the past or a pioneer of the future." —Deepak Chopra

Some people brood over their unpleasant past. They get into a negative zone and get depressed finally. Instead, they must look at the future with optimism. Research shows that people waste 30 percent of their precious time by thinking about their unpleasant past that cannot be changed. Hence, people must explore solutions for their problems. Their future solely depends on their mindset and the way they look at the world. They must start a new course on a clean slate. They must always think of 'what next' rather than 'what went wrong'. They must find out why and where things went wrong to learn lessons to become smarter and wiser. They must pioneer their future instead of becoming prisoners of their past.

When you observe the successful leaders including Abraham Lincoln, Mahatma Gandhi, and Nelson Mandela, they underwent lots of trials and tribulations. They did not look where they fell but they looked where they slipped and bounced back from their failures.

Tools to Avoid Becoming a Prisoner of the Past

Steve Jobs once remarked, "Your time is limited, so don't waste it living someone else's life. Don't be trapped by dogma which is living with the results of other people's thinking. Don't let the noise of others' opinions drown out your own inner voice. And most important, have the courage to follow your heart and intuition. They somehow already know what you truly want to become. Everything else is secondary." Here are some tools and techniques to avoid becoming a prisoner of the past:

- Let go off your unpleasant past. Focus on what you *can* do, not what you *cannot* do.
- Embrace uncertainty. Don't *react*, but *act* to the circumstances.
- Learn when to hold and when to fold. There is a thin line separating both. It requires immense judgment and intuition to decide when to hold and when to fold. Elon Musk remarked, "Persistence is very important. You should not give up unless you are forced to give up."
- When things go wrong repeatedly, lie low for a while and wait for an appropriate opportunity to make things fall into place.
- Ensure that you reorganize your body and brain constantly with your new experiences.
- Try meditation or yoga or go for regular physical exercises to energize your mind and body.
- Network with the right people.
- Have an attitude of gratitude.
- Look at the door that is opened.
- Fight for pretty things, not petty things.
- Look for possibilities, not impossibilities.
- Learn to make choices and commitments. Act keeping tomorrow in mind.

Remember, every dog has its own day. God throws challenges and offers opportunities to everybody. In fact, challenges test your abilities and enlarge your capabilities. Challenges unlock the leader in you. Hence, be bold to face the challenges. At the same time, be prepared all the time to explore opportunities.

Be an Architect of Your Future!

"The empires of the future are empires of the mind." —Winston Churchill

Life is a circus with ups and downs. Nobody can predict the future. However, you can pioneer your future with proper planning, preparation, and execution. Be mentally prepared for distractions and surprises. Align yourself whenever you are thrown out of gear with patience and perseverance to accomplish your goals and ambitions.

Fate is something happens automatically whereas destiny is something you create. Precisely, destiny is in your hands. To summarize, let bygones be bygones. Don't think about the unpleasant past that cannot be changed; and don't worry too much about the future that cannot be predicted. Instead, think about today which is in your hands. To conclude, don't be a prisoner of the past but be a pioneer of your future to make your life exciting. Life is great!

"The secret of change is to focus all of your energy, not on fighting the old, but on building the new." —Socrates

15 – Give Good to Get Good

"What is life?
Life is living in this moment, experiencing and experiment-
ing but experience isn't life.
Life is reflecting and meditating but reflection isn't life.
Life is helping and guiding but philanthropy isn't life.
Life is eating and drinking but food isn't life.
Life is reading and dancing but art isn't life.
Life is kissing and pleasuring but sex isn't life.
Life is winning and losing but competition isn't life.
Life is loving and caring but love isn't life.
Life is birthing and nurturing but children aren't life.
Life is letting go and surrendering but death isn't life.
Life is all these things but all these things aren't life.
Life is always more." —Kamand Kojouri

Life is an echo. If we do good things, we get back good things. If we do bad things we get back bad things. What goes around comes around. Here goes the famous story of a boy on 'hate and love.' A boy often complained to his mother that he hated the people. Mother advised him to go to the top of the hill and shout the same. The boy started to shout, "I hate you." He heard the response as "I hate you." He shouted louder and the echo got louder. Having vexed, he returned home and informed his mother that he heard the voice, "I hate you." Mother smiled and advised her son to go again and shout, "I love you." The boy went to the top of the hill and started to shout, "I love you." To his surprise, he heard the same response. He shouted louder and the echo got louder. He was excited, returned home and informed the same to his mother happily. The mother responded that life is an echo. If you do good, you get back the good. If you do bad, you get back bad. Hence, you must always do good to get good as what goes around comes around. Similarly, people across the globe must shed their cynicism and pessimism and start loving people with a positive attitude. In fact, attitude makes a huge difference. Hence, people must improve their attitude and love the people around them to enable the world to live with lots of love.

Enjoy Referent Power, not Positional Power

All religions encourage others to do good because 'as you sow, so shall you reap.' Treat others the way you want to be treated. Treat others with respect to earn respect. Some people enjoy power and prestige not because they hold any positional power but because they enjoy referent power. Referent power is the one that people enjoy without holding any high positions. They enjoy this power because of their good words and deeds, and the value they add to society. In contrast, positional power holds good as long as the people hold their positions and authority. The day they lose their position, they lose their power and prestige. People are intelligent to identify genuine and fake people. They respect people for their good deeds and words and for their charisma and character.

Conclusion

> "I'm a little pencil in the hand of a writing God, who is sending a love letter to the world." —Mother Teresa

If people understand the fact that what goes around comes around and life is an echo, most of the conflicts in the world will be resolved amicably. People become empathetic and think many times before making mistakes and crimes. To conclude, understand the fact that life is very short and make it sweet by keeping yourself happy and the people around you happy. Life is great!

> "Life is an echo. What you send out, comes back. What you sow, you reap. What you give, you get. What you see in others, exists in you. Remember, life is an echo. It always gets back to you. So give goodness." —Unknown

References

https://www.amazon.com/Soft-Leadership-Innovative-Negotiation-Prosperity/dp/1628655909

https://www.entrepreneur.com/slideshow/224215

16 – See Good in Others

"We can bring positive energy into our daily lives by smiling more, talking to strangers in line, replacing handshakes with hugs, and calling our friends just to tell them we love them." —Brandon Jenner

Once my elder son talked about a negative experience he had with one of my relatives. I asked him the reason for remembering the negative experience when the same person did so many good things to him since childhood. He had no answer for it. I told him that we must avoid remembering negative events in our lives. I further shared with him that we must forgive the individuals who harmed us; and forget negative events forever. Life is very short and we must know how to make it sweet. There is no room for ill-will and hatred against others. We must have a big heart to forgive people and forget unpleasant experiences to lead a happy and meaningful life.

I found many people often talking about their bad experiences rather than good experiences in their lives. There are some people who broke their precious relations due to silly reasons. We find married couple getting divorced due to their ego clashes, miscommunication, and negative experiences. Why don't they look at the positive aspects of an individual? Every Individual has both strengths and weaknesses. Why should we focus on the negative aspects of a personality? Why shouldn't we focus on the positive aspects of a personality?

The human mind captures negative aspects quicker than positive ones. When we view films, lots of violence and sex is shown, and people absorb such things faster than the positive ones. Hence, filmmakers and scriptwriters bombard with negativity to reach out to the audiences quickly. Here are some tools and techniques to convert your negative thinking into positive thinking:

- Surround yourself with positive people to create positive vibrations. Erin Heatherton righty remarked, "People like to be around those who give off positive energy."
- Don't brood over your unpleasant past which cannot be changed, and don't worry about the future that cannot be predicted. Learn to live in the present.
- Don't expect anything from others as people might not be in a position to help you always.
- Think of adding value to others.
- Have an attitude of gratitude. Thank God for gifting you a life in this world.

Zig Ziglar once remarked, "Positive thinking will let you do everything better than negative thinking will." Hence, think positive to do better in your life.

Mahatma Gandhi quoted, "A man is but the product of his thoughts. What he thinks, he becomes." Additionally, no person is entirely good and bad. Every person has both good and bad qualities. We must look at the positive side of an individual to build relations. We must strive to build bridges, not barriers. We can build a better world with love, peace, and harmony; when we see positive aspects in others. Remember, we are united by similarities but separated by differences.

There are several conflicts globally in the name of region, religion, caste, creed, ethnicity, nationality, and language because people see the negative aspects of others than the positive ones. There must be a change in the mindset and attitude of the people to build a better world. We must look at the door that is opened, not the one that is closed. We must look at the rising sun, not the setting sun to create a world which is full of hope and optimism.

"When you show deep empathy toward others, their defensive energy goes down, and positive energy replaces it. That's when you can get more creative in solving problems." —Stephen Covey

Good People are Rare to Get in this World!

"A great leader needs to love and respect people, and he needs to be comfortable with himself and with the world. He also needs to be able to forgive himself and others. In other words, a leader needs grace." —Leo Hindery Jr.

I have come across many people in my life who take their kith and kin for granted. They also take good people around them for granted. At times, they exploit good people with their selfish motives. I wanted to share a few thoughts on this topic.

Presently it is rare to find good people globally as most people are selfish. They often think of adding value to them, not to others. If you find people who think of adding value to others, respect them and encourage them to build a better world. Life is very short and nobody takes away the wealth at the time of death. Leave a good legacy. Make a difference. When you depart this world, you either leave with a good reputation or a bad reputation. Why don't you leave with a good reputation? Why don't you live with values? Why don't you leave a good leadership legacy? Remember, there is always a victory for values, not for people who cut corners and look for short-term gains.

I have come across a professional who worked in the publishing industry. I signed an agreement with the prestigious publishing company to publish my book in India in 2011. The person who worked in the company left the organization. Another person took over who stood by the commitment and published the book in 2012. He said, "Institutions are more important than individuals. Individuals come and go but the institutions survive. We must keep the objectives of institutions as paramount irrespective of the disagreement we have with our colleagues." On the other hand, I had a bitter experience with an eminent publisher in India with whom I signed my book proposal in 2010. The people who worked and the people responsible for clearing my book proposal left the organization. A new team arrived and created their clauses and canceled my agreement. I felt bad about the organization for betraying me.

I am still in touch with the publisher who cleared my book proposal because of his commitment and value system. I have forgotten many people who have cheated me. But I still remember that person for his commitment and ethical values. To conclude, if you get good people in your life, keep them close to your heart. Don't take them for granted. Good people are rare to find in this world. Don't undermine them just because they are close to you. Don't take them for granted just because they are easily available in front of you. Remember, you never know the value of what you have until you lose it.

"Good manners are essential. No matter what the message, the situation, we listen and respond with respect and, always good manners." —Frances Hesselbein

17 – Achieve Success with Integrity—A Father's Message to his Son

"No love is greater than that of a father for His son." — Dan Brown, *Angels & Demons*

When my son, Ramakrishna Sayee was leaving America for higher education in August 2016, he asked me to offer some suggestions. I shared with him, "Eat well. Exercise every day. Earn qualification. Earn money ethically and legally. Enjoy your life."

Every father wants his children to do well to enable his next generation to lead a better and comfortable life. He wants his children to do well in their spheres and add value to themselves and to society. However, very few children take their father's advice and suggestions seriously and positively. The children who take advice from their parents seriously will achieve amazing success in their lives.

Fathers are always protective about their children the way the mothers are protective about their children. The only difference between the mother and the father is that the latter rarely expresses his emotions and feelings while the former exhibits her love and affection toward her children openly. In fact, a father must be firm and filled with fun toward his children while a mother must love and care for her children. There are several differences between their roles and responsibilities.

It is observed that a father's contribution is often less recognized than a mother's contribution. It is because the mother takes care of her children and serves food regularly. She invests her time in upbringing them. Hence, she connects with her children quickly. In contrast, the father goes outside to earn money to ensure livelihood for his family. He earns bread and keeps things ready in the pipeline to provide everything on the platter at home. At times, a father is supposed to be firm at home to ensure that things fall into place which may not be appreciated by their children who are often fun-loving. Hence, a father's contribution often goes unrecognized. It is also observed that the daughter loves her father more, and the son loves her mother more.

William Bennett once remarked, "Real fatherhood means love and commitment and sacrifice and a willingness to share responsibility and not walking away from one's children." A father aspires to become a role model for his children. However, every father has some flaws. At times, children look at flaws in their father rather than the contribution he makes to his family.

Only when you become a successful father or mother at home, you will be able to become a successful leader in the workplace. Remember, real leadership starts from your home.

True fathers take a great interest in the upbringing of their children. They teach how to ride a bike, learn swimming, play games, read good books, write articles and speak well. They constantly care and guide their children. They groom their children as leaders. Despite resistance from children, they don't give up their responsibility to groom their children as well-rounded personalities. They impart education and emphasize character-building. They prefer sharing their knowledge to sharing their wealth. They prepare their children to face challenges in their lives. Whenever their children fail and fall, they handhold and keep them on the right track and fast-track.

Message to my Son

Son,
Surround with good books to improve your knowledge and with positive friends to grow as a healthy citizen to

add value to society. There is no free lunch in the world. Remember, everything comes at a price. Success comes from struggles and sacrifices. You must work hard to prove yourself in this cut-throat competitive world. You must identify your passions and pursue them relentlessly. Focus on your passionate area and strive hard for a minimum of 10 years to establish yourself. Don't be overjoyed by short-term success. Don't get complacent. Remember, who wins at the end of life race counts, not who wins in the middle of life journey. Don't flight but fight to the finish. Be resilient. Don't become a servant to technology. Ensure that technology becomes your servant.

Travel as often as you can. Traveling teaches tolerance because you come across diversified communities and cultures when you travel. When I served in the Indian Air Force, I volunteered to travel and I traveled entire India in various aircrafts including Mi17 helicopter. I learned a lot, and I share my experiences with others during my leadership development training programs. Remember, to travel is to lead.

Respect women. Empower them. Handhold them to enable them to lead from the front. Build bridges, not barriers. Don't react, act. Connect with likeminded people. Build trust in others. Remember that trust is earned, not given. Serve others. Be a giver. Add value to others. Respect all cultures and communities. Love your mother but don't hate another person's mother. Love your nation but don't hate another person's nation.

Don't blame the circumstances. Never criticize, complain and condemn others. Start from where you are, and with what you have. Follow your heart. Follow your passion. You have only one life to accomplish your ambitions. Life is very short. Hence, make it sweet. Explore ideas for issues. Emphasize ideas, not individuals. Cut the cloth as per the coat. Be frugal, not cheap. Have the attitude of gratitude.

Maintain a journal of 'to do' list to manage your time and stay focused on your goals clearly. Remember, if you waste one second you have wasted one second of your precious life. Learn from everyone without any ego. No man is entirely good and no man is entirely bad because every good man has some flaws and every bad man has some great traits. Hence, look for the good in others by ignoring the bad. Forget your unpleasant events and forgive others. Character counts, not charisma. Strive for excellence, not perfection. Emphasize "means", not "ends." Achieve success with integrity. Failure is only a comma, not a full stop. Work for satisfaction, not for recognition. Learn continuously. Share your knowledge with others. Make a difference in their lives.

Love, Dad

Conclusion

"The most important thing a father can do for his children is to love their mother." —Theodore Hesburgh

A father must provide good education and build character in his children. Giving away wealth to children will not bring permanent peace but it can only give temporary prosperity. An ideal father must build confidence in his children to encounter the challenges squarely to come out with flying colors. Life is not a cakewalk. Life is beautiful! Life is great!

"I knew my father had done the best he could, and I had no regrets about the way I'd turned out. Regrets about journey, maybe, but not the destination." —Nicholas Sparks, *The Notebook*

Note: This message is not only to my son but all global youth to inculcate a positive attitude to achieve success with integrity and make their parents and nations proud.

18 – Harness the Power of Social Media to Spread Spiritualism

"Our scientific power has outrun our spiritual power. We have guided missiles and misguided men." —Martin Luther King, Jr.

When I posted a quote on love and relationships on social media platforms, one of the visitors has commented that the digital world has brought down the relations between the people due to lack of physical connectivity. I outlined this aspect when I wrote an article on the importance of social media. However, I did not have the opportunity to elaborate on the importance of human relations and spirituality vis-à-vis social media. Let us discuss the role of social media, spirituality and human relations in this chapter.

Significance of Social Media

"Being human in the digital world is about building a digital world for humans." —Andrew Keen

Social media has changed the face of the world. It has converted the world into a small village. People interact with others on social media and access the information easily. They connect and disconnect with others easily. Social networking site such as Facebook has revolutionized the world because it has become a democratic platform for the people to voice their views and brand themselves. Previously people approached print media to voice their views. Currently, they post their views on Facebook to get noticed quickly. The professional networking site especially LinkedIn has revolutionized the world to network with professionals. Viveka von Rosen remarked, "LinkedIn is a channel to increase, not a tool to replace, your networking efforts, and it is an excellent vehicle to facilitate some facets of your marketing and business strategies." It offers several opportunities including employment and branding. It allows people to post their views and publish their articles. Previously people chased eminent publications to get their articles published. With LinkedIn providing such an amazing opportunity, people started posting their articles to get their knowledge disseminated quickly. The LinkedIn editors promptly pick up the articles that go viral quickly, categorize and promote them thus enhancing the visibility for the posts increasing the dissemination of knowledge. Previously people enjoyed reading print editions. However, they appreciate reading digital editions presently. People prefer digital books to print books currently. What a tremendous transformation the social media has brought!

Undoubtedly, technology has changed the world rapidly in the last decade. Previously, there was a scarcity of information. Presently people find it difficult to choose the right information as they are inundated with excessive information. Previously people retained huge information. Presently people have short attention spans. Likewise, there are several ways social media has influenced and changed the mindsets and attitudes of the people globally. People want to date with others digitally. They want instant love, romance, and sex. They must be very careful about what they post on social media because once the content goes viral, it cannot be withdrawn. Above all, there is hardly any secrecy in the digital world. Angela Merkel rightly remarked, "The digital world creates a situation where there are no secrets anymore."

Social Media Takes You to a Fantasy and Fantastic World!

The social media takes you to a virtual world where people thrive with excitement temporarily. Most of the relations are artificial and commercial. Nobody clearly knows the challenges of others because people don't know each other physically. People often compare and contrast with others assuming that others' lead better lives which may not be the reality. It is rightly remarked that another's pasture always looks greener. At times, they compare with the successful people. They hardly realize how much pain the successful people have taken to reach such positions. Some people want to network with eminent people on social media which may not be possible always. Once they are back from the virtual world to the physical world, they find it difficult to cope up with the realities. It is like going to a film, and be in an imaginative world for a while and reverting to the real-life after viewing the film.

Social networking helps communicate with others and make friends but the communication and friendships may not be as reliable as the physical ones.

When televisions came people began viewing it thus breaking physical association with neighbors and others. When smartphones came people began communicating virtually thus breaking physical communication. We must wed technology but to what extent we must wed technology is a matter of debate. It is shocking to note that the wife and husband who love together and live together in the home chat through smartphones rather than physically. It is a well-admitted fact that televisions invaded homes previously, and smartphones invaded bedrooms presently.

Use Technology Wisely

"Technology is permeating every single thing we do...And to the extent that we can better expose our young people to all the different ways that technology can be used, not just for video games or toys, we're planning for the future." —Marc Morial

Digital pressure is worse than physical pressure because the former deals with the mind while the latter deals with the body. When the mind is stressed it loses its balance. Hence, it is essential to minimize digital pressure by controlling its usage. People often talk about meditation, yoga, and mindfulness because of the pressures the technology has brought to the people. When people are digitally disconnected they enjoy their life happily. It doesn't mean that we must throw technology altogether. We must know how to use technology because technology is a double-edged sword. It is both a boon and bane, and it all depends on how we use it. Similarly, social media is both a boon and bane. It all depends on how you use it. If you use it constructively, you can build a better world. In contrast, if you use it destructively, you can divide the people and create havoc in the world. If the knife is in the hands of a thief, he could use for destructive purpose. If the same knife is in the hands of a surgeon, he could save the life of a person.

Harness the Power of Social Media

"Engage, Enlighten, Encourage and especially…just be yourself! Social media is a community effort, everyone is an asset." —Susan Cooper

Elif Safak remarked, "The digital world is developing with such force and such a pace that you simply can't ban or control it. People want to be globally connected." As times and technologies are changing rapidly, we must change accordingly because change is the only thing constant in this world. We must learn how to use social media successfully to spread spiritualism in the world. Instead of treating social media as an enemy, we must treat it as an ally to spread spiritualism and promote fraternity in the world.

I effectively use social media to share my knowledge with the world. My vision is to build a knowledgeable global society. I have four blogs and share my ideas and insights. I also post articles on LinkedIn and share the links on social media platforms including

Facebook, and Twitter. I basically write posts on leadership, ethics, and success. Recently I have included spiritualism in my writings because I want to replace religion with love to build a better world. Hence, we must make use of social media judiciously to bring the change and make a difference to society.

Conclusion

"I've created a narrative of the world. I live in the world – tenuously, most times. I've avoided the digital world." — James Ellroy

Although humans created robots, it appears that technology has converted humans into robots. The trend needs to be checked for the benefit of humankind. Remember, technology is both a culprit and catalyst. It all depends on how judiciously we use it to transform society.

It is a well-admitted fact that human relations cannot be replaced by digital relations because digital relations give temporary excitement while human relations give permanent happiness. People appreciate permanent happiness, not the so-called temporary excitement which is often found to be fake. Hence, emphasize connecting with the people physically rather than virtually to lead a happy and meaningful life.

To summarize, it is regrettable to note that virtual relations have replaced traditional human relations. People find it comfortable to send messages than to meet physically. It is not good in the long run as it brings not only health hazards complications but also human complications. To conclude, encourage human relations over virtual relations to bring peace, happiness, and joy.

"If we are to go forward, we must go back and rediscover those precious values – that all reality hinges on moral foundations and that all reality has spiritual control." —Martin Luther King, Jr.

19 – ADD VALUE TO SOCIETY THROUGH PHILANTHROPY

"Effective philanthropy requires a lot of time and creativity – the same kind of focus and skills that building a business requires." —Bill Gates

Globally renowned entrepreneurs including Warren Buffett (The Giving Pledge), Mario Batali (The Mario Batali Foundation), Craig Newmark (Craigconnects.org), Michael Bloomberg (Bloomberg Philanthropies), Mark Zuckerberg (Newark New Jersey Public Schools), Tony Hawk (The Tony Hawk Foundation), Marc Benioff (UCSF Foundation), Oprah Winfrey (Angel Network), and Sean Parker (Charity: Water) have made an immense difference to the society through their charity and philanthropy. Andrew Carnegie once remarked, "No man can become rich without himself enriching others. The man who dies rich dies disgraced."

Philanthropy and Charity

Philanthropy is to give wealth back to the society especially to the less fortunate. It is different from charity. Philanthropy involves the active involvement of the giver and stakeholders while the charity doesn't involve any active involvement and engagement of the giver. The giver gives his wealth to bodies that take care of the philanthropic activities. Eli Broad rightly differentiated, "Charity is just writing checks and not being engaged. Philanthropy, to me, is being engaged, not only with your resources but getting people and yourself really involved and doing things that haven't been done before."

A Striking Story on Philanthropy

"What we have done for ourselves alone dies with us; what we have done for others and the world remains and is immortal." —Albert Pike

Nobody brings anything to the world at the time of birth and takes back anything from this world at the time of death. What one can do is to grow rich personally, professionally and socially and share the riches to the less fortunate during the lifetime. Here goes the story of an entrepreneur who was very rich and donated his entire money to charity. He was a self-made man with a rags-to-riches inspiring story. When he decided to share his entire wealth to the society from where he received the wealth, one of his friends questioned him for not sharing his wealth with his two sons. He replied as follows: If my children are capable they will earn money by themselves. In that case, I don't have to share my wealth with them. If my children are incapable they will destroy the entire wealth that I share with them. In that case, there is no meaning to share my wealth with them. It is obvious from this story that we must make our children competent and independent to enable them to work hard and smart to earn money. It gives them a sense of satisfaction and meaning in their lives. And people will not have any opportunity to point out that the children enjoy the wealth given away by their parents. John Maxwell rightly remarked, "If you do everything for your children, what will they do for themselves."

Impart Education and Character to Children

Education and character are the two things parents must provide to their children. If they are educated, they can lead to any part of the world with courage and confidence. They can earn their livelihood and provide meaning to their lives. If they are imparted with character, they will live with dignity and honor and achieve success with integrity. Hence, parents must provide education and character to their children instead of sharing their wealth. In this way, they bring up their children in the right way and add value to society. At the same time, educational institutions must impart moral education to students to enable them to grow as healthy citizens.

Emphasize Character Education

"People of character do the right thing, not because they think it will change the world but because they refuse to be changed by the world." —Michael Josephson

Most students work hard and smart to acquire educational qualifications. They often compete with their colleagues to stand out. One degree they must acquire is 'character degree'. Other degrees don't have any value if they are not equipped with this character degree.

Most students aspire to acquire educational qualifications to grab employment opportunities. These qualifications are essential to obtain employment. If they have character degree, they get enlightened and empowered throughout their lives. They can grow as healthy citizens to build a healthy nation and a healthy global society.

Billy Graham once remarked, "When wealth is lost, nothing is lost; when health is lost, something is lost; when character is lost, all is lost." That is the importance of character! Therefore, your character is your asset. Like education, your character cannot be taken away by others unless you agree to lose it. You can acquire anything and everything under the sun on the earth if you have a strong character. You can earn your lost money, lost happiness, and lost peace; if you have a strong character.

In leadership, people often talk about charisma. But what people must learn is to emphasize on character, not charisma. Charisma may give temporary popularity which is like a passing cloud. What character gives you is a permanent place in the hearts of the people beyond your lifetime far above these passing clouds to shine like a star forever.

Achieve Success with Integrity

Some students aspire to achieve success by hook or crook due to peer pressure and age pressure. The success achieved through wrongful means will not sustain whereas success achieved through rightful means will ensure your longevity. Additionally, it helps you command respect and become a role model and legend.

Elmer G. Letterman quoted, "Personality can open doors, but only character can keep them open." To keep their doors open, students must emphasize on character degrees than on paper degrees that serve as a foothold to be placed permanently in companies. Although paper degrees provide them as a platform to enter employment, it is the character degree that provides them a permanent platform to ensure employability. It may be easy to be appreciated but tough to be respected by others. Success may be appreciated by others but when success achieved with integrity will be respected by others. Hence, strive to achieve success with integrity by equipping with a character degree.

Role of Educators

Educators must impart character education to students to check declining ethical values among students. Educators are the true academic leaders who build a society by imparting character education to students. Students must take interest to acquire character because the character cannot just be taught in the classroom. What educators can do is to inspire students to acquire character. Ultimately, it is the students who must show interest to acquire it based on their values and virtues.

Role of Parents

Parents must take responsibility. They must spend some time regularly with their children at home to connect with them to build a strong value system. They must prepare their children to face challenges in life. They must teach their children to emphasize character education rather than paper qualifications. Character education helps throughout their lives whereas paper qualifications serve for a short period. Parents must not be in a mad race to apply pressure on their children to acquire scores and grades in exams. They must encourage curricular and extracurricular activities apart from inspiring them to acquire character education. They must set an example to their children at home, and educators must set an example in educational institutions to impart the right values and virtues among students. In fact, both parents and educators must take collective responsibility in this regard. Educational institutions must emphasize the overall development of students rather than the partial performance of grades and scores. Hence, there must be coordinated efforts from all stakeholders including educators, parents, students, and educational institutions to impart character education to students.

Anne Frank once remarked, "Parents can only give good advice or put them on the right paths, but the final forming of a person's character lies in their own hands." Therefore, the final onus lies with students to choose the right values and virtues to acquire character degrees.

This advice may bring discomfort to some of the ambitious students. But it is worth waiting to achieve success with integrity. The intention is to inspire students to dream big to shine like stars with character education rather than to become passing clouds with their paper qualifications.

Lead by Example

"Philanthropy is almost the only virtue which is sufficiently appreciated by mankind." —Henry David Thoreau

The educators in educational institutions must take initiative to impart moral education. The parents at home must impart value system by leading with example. Currently, the technology is highly advanced and the children ape the negative things rather than the positive things. It is a fact that people accept negativity more than positivity. Additionally, children are much smarter than their parents due to the influence of their peers and technology. The peer pressure plays a crucial role either to make or break the children. Hence, parents must keep a vigil on their children and ensure that they are surrounded by positive and healthy friends. To conclude, emphasize moral education to children to enable them to grow as healthy and global citizens. It helps them achieve success with integrity and inculcates in them giving back to the society to build a better world.

> "Philanthropy is commendable, but it must not cause the philanthropist to overlook the circumstances of economic injustice which make philanthropy necessary." —Martin Luther King, Jr.

Reference
https://www.entrepreneur.com/slideshow/224215

20 – Practice Yoga to Lead a Happy and Healthy Life

"The meaning of our self is not to be found in its separateness from God and others, but in the ceaseless realization of yoga, of union." —Rabindranath Tagore

The famous people including David Beckham, Jessica Biel, Jennifer Aniston, Russell Brand, Ricky Martin, Meg Ryan, Jennifer Aniston, Kate Hudson, Gisele Bundchen, Lady Gaga, Madonna, Jeremy Piven, Beyonce, Tom Hanks, and Alessandra Ambrosio practice yoga. It is obvious from these examples that yoga is widely practiced globally. Yoga has its origins from India and has been an intrinsic part of the Indian ethos for over 5,000 years. Patanjali is regarded as the father of Yoga. The United Nations celebrates June 21st of every year as an 'International Yoga Day.' India's Prime Minister Narendra Modi said, "International Yoga Day is not the brainchild of a government or of the United Nations. It is a reflection of the largest knowledge-based peoples' movement the world has ever seen…We will take this movement forward to aim for better health, more fulfilled lives and more connected communities." In this chapter, we will discuss yoga and its benefits and applications to bring wellness and happiness.

What is Yoga?
Yoga is an ancient physical and mental practice. It is not connected with any religion. It is practiced in varying forms and styles but

generally consists of four main practices[13]—physical exercise (poses or "asana"), relaxation, meditation, and breathing techniques (pranayama). The word 'Yoga' originated from the Sanskrit word 'Yuj' which means to yoke or bind. It is referred to as "union" or a method of discipline. There are four main paths of Yoga[14] — Karma Yoga, Bhakti Yoga, Raja Yoga, and Jnana Yoga. Each is suited to a different temperament or approach to life. All the paths lead ultimately to the same destination – to union with Brahman or God – and the lessons of each of them need to be integrated if true wisdom is to be attained. There are several types of yoga and one of them is Hatha yoga[15] which integrates three elements: physical poses, called asanas; controlled breathing practiced in conjunction with asanas; and a short period of deep relaxation or meditation. Yoga[16] encourages practitioners to learn various breathing exercises, including deep abdominal breathing, the three-part breath and lengthening the exhalation to mention a few. It is widely followed in the West. There is often confusion between yoga and meditation. Meditation is mainly about the mind while yoga is mainly about the body. Of course, practicing yoga ultimately leads to mental and holistic development. Sri Sri Ravi Shankar rightly remarked, "Yoga is not just exercise and asanas. It is the emotional integration and spiritual elevation with a touch of mystic element, which gives you a glimpse of something beyond all imagination."

Merits of Yoga

"Health is not a mere absence of disease. It is a dynamic expression of life – in terms of how joyful, loving and enthusiastic you are." —Sri Sri Ravi Shankar

---

13 http://www.bwy.org.uk/newtoyoga

14 http://www.sivananda.org/teachings/fourpaths.html

15 http://www.health.harvard.edu/mind-and-mood/yoga-for-anxiety-and-depression

16 https://www.ncbi.nlm.nih.gov/pmc/articles/PMC2997232/

Yoga is essential in the current complex world where people are stressed out. It has innumerable advantages. It helps overcome volatility, uncertainty, complexity, and ambiguity. It improves organizational performance and productivity thus achieving organizational excellence and effectiveness. Most organizations realized its importance and integrated into their corporate training programs. Some global organizations integrated yoga in their organizational culture to keep employees happy and productive. Individually, yoga decreases stress and improves performance of mind and body. It is rightly remarked that the body is the temple of the mind. Yoga keeps body agile and active. It fills your mind with energy and enthusiasm. It leads to longevity and keeps you free from diseases and ailments in old age. Yoga master, B. K. S. Iyengar rightly remarked, "Daily practice of yoga will keep old age at bay. It enables us to endure what cannot be cured and makes the entire cycle of life worth living." It compartmentalizes activities in life and offers you inner strength. It helps discover the right path and accomplish goals easily. It improves concentration and enhances focus, patience, and perseverance. It leads to work-life balance. Precisely, yoga is the passport to health and happiness, and a means to wellness and happiness. India's Prime Minister Narendra Modi said, "The problems of modern lifestyles are well known. People suffer from stress-related ailments, lifestyle-related diseases like diabetes and hypertension. We have found ways to control communicable diseases, but the burden of disease is shifting to non-communicable diseases. Young people who are not at peace with themselves seek refuge in drugs and alcohol. There is ample evidence that practicing yoga helps combat stress and chronic conditions. If the body is a temple of the mind, yoga creates a beautiful temple."

Yoga and Health Benefits

"The success of Yoga does not lie in the ability to perform postures but in how it positively changes the way we live our life and our relationships." —T.K.V. Desikachar

Research[17] shows that yoga can bring many benefits. Here are some benefits of practicing yoga. It effectively improves the osteoarthritis of the hand. It improves some subjective symptoms in asthma sufferers. It effectively treats chronic low back pain and some of its side effects. A study shows that practicing yoga is more effective than physical therapy at reducing pain, anxiety, and depression, and improving spinal mobility. Yoga benefits those with cancer. It helps people overcome depression. It reduces the risk factors for diabetes and cardiovascular disease in healthy people. It improves cognitive function and perceived stress during the menopause. It effectively combats stress and burnout. It has a positive effect on overweight women with problems with binge eating. And it benefits women both before and during giving birth. Here are some more advantages of practicing yoga: Yoga improves your body flexibility and builds your muscle strength. It strengthens your spine and improves your body posture. It improves your bone density, increases your blood flow, and immunity. It improves your heart rate and lowers blood sugar. It improves your nervous system and releases tension in your limbs. It keeps allergies and viruses away. It improves your love life and relationships. It increases your self-esteem and self-confidence. Above all, it develops the attitude of gratitude. Yogi Bhajan rightly remarked, "The attitude of gratitude is the highest yoga." Yoga helps you achieve a good appetite, free motion and sound sleep which are the symptoms of wellness and happiness.

Yoga in Global Organizations

Yoga has invited huge attention globally with the global companies realizing its importance. They started to invest money in their learning and development programs. With the rapid growth in technology, people encounter several diseases and ailments both mentally and physically. Hence, most people find that yoga is the solution to their problems.

---

17 http://www.bwy.org.uk/pdf/BWY_Sheffield_Presentation-Feb13.pdf

How to Perform Yoga?

"Yoga is 99 percent practice and one percent theory." —Sri Pattabhi Jois

You can do yoga at your home or office. You can do either indoor or outdoor. You can do it alone or with others. All that you need is a mat to do it unlike other games and activities such as gymnastics, athletics, and aerobics that need expensive equipment and materials. For performing yoga, there is no need for playgrounds, swimming pool or gyms. You must do it with an empty stomach. You can fix at any time as per your comfort during the day. You must wear comfortable clothes to do it. Ensure that the place you do yoga is serene and peaceful. Initially do it at the supervision of yoga teacher, if possible. Or you may view the video clippings of experts doing yoga. Start slowly with comfortable "asanas" and gradually switch over to difficult ones. Begin with a positive mindset that you can do it. While performing yoga, focus on your breathing and your movement to achieve the desired outcomes.

Yoga is not like taking pills to get the desired results. Yoga needs your time and efforts. It doesn't need much investment. You can do yoga at any age. However, it is advisable to do it with the supervision of an expert or teacher to achieve the desired outcomes. Consult your doctor, if you have major health complications.

Conclusion

"This world is your body. This world is a great school, This world is your silent teacher." —Swami Sivananda

Yoga brings the world together by connecting the human race without any regional, cultural, linguistic, ethnic and national barriers. It is a means for your wellness and happiness. Yoga is India's gift to the world. To conclude, understand the importance of yoga and practice it regularly to achieve peace, happiness and all-round success in your life.

"The practice of Yoga brings us face to face with the extraordinary complexity of our own being." —Sri Aurobindo

References

http://www.bwy.org.uk/newtoyoga

http://www.bwy.org.uk/pdf/BWY_Sheffield_Presentation-Feb13.pdf

http://www.sivananda.org/teachings/fourpaths.html

http://www.health.harvard.edu/mind-and-mood/yoga-for-anxiety-and-depression

https://www.ncbi.nlm.nih.gov/pmc/articles/PMC2997232/

http://timesofindia.indiatimes.com/india/Yoga-is-our-collective-gift-to-humanity-PM-Modi/articleshow/47762520.cms

21 – Make Peace Education a Philosophy

"Power properly understood is nothing but the ability to achieve purpose. It is the strength required to bring about social, political and economic change. ... What is needed is a realization that power without love is reckless and abusive, and love without power is sentimental and anemic. Power at its best is love implementing the demands of justice, and justice at its best is power correcting everything that stands against love." —Martin Luther King, Jr.

Globally several soldiers die due to wars and conflicts. The families of the soldiers undergo mental agony and trauma, and the respective nations lose their precious human resources and productivity. Hence, there is an urgent need to emphasize peace education globally to avert conflicts and wars; and to promote peace and prosperity. In this chapter, we will discuss the importance of peace education to nations to achieve global stability and prosperity.

The United Nations observes International Day of Peace every year on September 21, 2013. For the first time in 2013, it exclusively dedicated the year to education. Hague Appeal for Peace Global Campaign for Peace Education declares, "A culture of peace will be achieved when citizens of the world understand global problems, have the skills to resolve conflicts and struggle for justice non-violently, live by international standards of human rights and equity, appreciate cultural diversity, and respect the Earth and each other. Such learning can only be achieved with systematic education for peace."

What is Peace Education?

"Peace does not mean an absence of conflicts; differences will always be there. Peace means solving these differences through peaceful means; through dialogue, education, knowledge; and through humane ways." —Dalai Lama XIV

Peace education can be defined as the process of acquiring education emphasizing human values, principles, ethics, and etiquette. It emphasizes humanity and respects dignity and diversity by looking at similarities, not differences. Peace education in UNICEF[18] refers to the process of promoting the knowledge, skills, attitudes, and values needed to bring about behavior changes that will enable children, youth and adults to prevent conflict and violence, both overt and structural; to resolve conflict peacefully; and to create the conditions conducive to peace, whether at an intrapersonal, interpersonal, intergroup, national or international level.

James Page suggests peace education be thought of as "encouraging a commitment to peace as a settled disposition and enhancing the confidence of the individual as an individual agent of peace; as informing the student on the consequences of war and social injustice; as informing the student on the value of peaceful and just social structures and working to uphold or develop such social structures; as encouraging the student to love the world and to imagine a peaceful future; and as caring for the student and encouraging the student to care for others."

Research shows that seven soldiers commit suicide in America every day. Over 100 military personnel commit suicide every year

---

18 https://www.unicef.org/education/files/PeaceEducation.pdf

in India. Depression is taking over the world. Stress in soldiers is at an alarming rate, and there is an urgent need for peace education with an emphasis on spiritualism. It is essential to offer counseling sessions and conduct yoga, meditation, and equip them with soft skills to enhance their morale.

Importance of Peace Education

"If the human race wishes to have a prolonged and indefinite period of material prosperity, they have only got to behave in a peaceful and helpful way toward one another."
—Winston Churchill

The way the world needs moral education and character education, the world needs peace education currently. It must start from the primary education level to enable children to understand and adopt it. Mahatma Gandhi rightly remarked, "If we are to create peace in the world, we must begin with the children." Additionally, the United Nations[19] has called on every country to 'ensure that children, from an early age, benefit from education to enable them to resolve any dispute peacefully and in a spirit of respect for human dignity and of tolerance.'

Educational institutions must emphasize developing the right attitude through peace education. They must highlight the problems and costs involved in conflicts and violence. Apart from life skills and soft skills, children must be taught on peace education from the primary education level itself. They must be taught on diversity and dignity. There are innumerable advantages of imparting peace education. It avoids conflicts and eliminates violence. It shuns violence. It resolves conflicts amicably. It encourages fraternity and camaraderie to live people with amity and goodwill.

---

19 http://peace-education.org.uk/why-education-for-peace-is-important

Course Curriculum for Peace Education

"Establishing lasting peace is the work of education." — Maria Montessori

Here is the course curriculum on peace education which can be customized as per the local and global needs: An ideal peace education can be divided into three categories—knowledge, skills, and attitudes. The following topics can be considered under the category of knowledge—awareness of own needs, self awareness, understanding nature of conflict and peace, ability to identify causes of conflict, and non-violent means of resolution, conflict analysis, enhancing knowledge of community, mechanisms for building peace and resolving conflict, mediation process, understanding of rights and responsibilities, understanding interdependence between individuals and societies, awareness of cultural heritage, and recognition of prejudice.

The following topics can be considered under the category of skills—communication, active listening, self-expression, paraphrasing, reframing, assertiveness, ability to cooperate, affirmation, critical thinking, ability to think critically about prejudice, ability to deal with stereotypes, dealing with emotions, problem-solving, ability to generate alternative solutions, constructive conflict resolution, conflict prevention, participation in society on behalf of peace, and ability to live with change.

The following topics can be considered under the category of attitudes—self-respect, positive self-image, strong self-concept, tolerance, acceptance of others, respect for differences, respect for rights and responsibilities of children and parents, bias awareness, gender equity, empathy, reconciliation, solidarity, social responsibility, sense of justice and equality, and joy in living.

Make Peace Education a Philosophy

"Peace is a daily, a weekly, a monthly process, gradually changing opinions, slowly eroding old barriers, quietly building new structures." —John F. Kennedy

The need of the hour is to impart peace education globally. The nations must invest a significant amount of money, time and resources on peace education rather than on prison education. In fact, lots of money is spent on prisons than on peace currently. Wars result in increased taxes. The world cannot afford nuclear wars and the Third World War. Peace is the only way to ensure global stability and prosperity. It requires support from all stakeholders including parents, educators, educational institutions, NGOs, government and global society to ensure global stability and prosperity. To conclude, impart peace education and make peace education a philosophy to build a better world.

"No one is born hating another person because of the color of his skin, or his background, or his religion. People must learn to hate, and if they can learn to hate, they can be taught to love, for love comes more naturally to the human heart than its opposite." —Nelson Mandela

References

https://www.unicef.org/education/files/PeaceEducation.pdf

http://peace-education.org.uk/why-education-for-peace-is-important

https://www.amazon.com/Promoting-Peace-Through-International-Law/dp/0198722737

22 – Emphasize the Philosophy of 'Health First, Education Second, and Wealth Third'

"I have the audacity to believe that peoples everywhere can have three meals a day for their bodies, education and culture for their minds, and dignity, equality and freedom for their spirits." —Martin Luther King, Jr.

In this concluding chapter, we will discuss uncertainty, happiness, spiritual education, humanity, and the philosophy of 'health first, education second, and wealth third.'

Experience Uncertainty

"Uncertainty is the only certainty there is, and knowing how to live with insecurity is the only security." —John Allen Paulos

Life is full of uncertainty. Nobody can predict what happens next. Most people are scared of uncertainty and worried about their future. They must understand that uncertainty is an integral part of life. They must embrace uncertainty to lead their life by realizing, adjusting and leading from the front. Sadhguru Jaggi Vasudev remarked, "Every uncertainty is a new possibility. It is just one's inability to handle new terrain that makes one conclude that something is uncertain." He added, "Do what you want but the world won't be the way you want it to be. Forget about the world, even people in your family won't be the way you want them to be. The best way to handle uncertainty is to see reality for what it is. There are no problems. There are only situations, some you know how to handle and some you don't know how to handle. What is a problem for one person is an opportunity for another."

To embrace uncertainty, understand the ground realities, improve your attitude to reconcile with them, and build your competencies and capabilities accordingly. Sid Mohasseb remarked in *The Caterpillars Edge*, "To realize an improved future you must purposefully leave the past behind, and embrace the uncertainty ahead—constantly and without fear. You must evolve, then evolve again and thrive."

Treat Uncertainty as a Friend, not a Foe

"The quality of your life is in direct proportion to the amount of uncertainty you can comfortably deal with." —Tony Robbins

Treat uncertainty as a friend, not a foe. It is an exciting experience because we don't know what happens next. Entrepreneurs, adventurers, and explorers thrive on uncertainty. It gives them energy and enthusiasm to rise high in life. It is like taking a risk. Remember, not to take a risk is also a risk. Life is worth living when it has challenges. Hence, take risks and enjoy the uncertainty to provide meaning to your life.

Happiness Lies within, not Outside

"Thousands of candles can be lighted from a single candle, and the life of the candle will not be shortened. Happiness never decreases by being shared." —Buddha

Ideally, any nation's growth is measured by its economic development. However, the tiny remote Himalayan kingdom of Bhutan is an exception where it first invented the idea of using happiness as a measure of good governance. It coined 'Gross National Happiness' index thus becoming a trendsetter to other nations globally. Many nations are taking a leaf out of Bhutan to keep their people happy. Bhutanese are less materialistic and lead a contented life. They don't get into the rat race in the name of development.

Nations adopt Gross Domestic Product (GDP) but Bhutan adopted "Gross National Happiness" (GNH) in 1972. It was proposed by Jigme Singye Wangchuck, the country's former king and the father of the present king, Jigme Khesar Namgyel Wangchuck. This new perspective put Bhutan on the global map. Bhutan became the benchmark for happiness globally. GDP measures the economic health of a country while GNH measures the happiness of a country.

Previously companies emphasized the slogan of 'customers first, employees second, and shareholders third'. But presently companies emphasize 'employees first, customers second, and shareholders third'. In a similar spirit, a nation's wellbeing must be measured by people's happiness rather than by so-called economic development. Only when people are happy, they will be able to contribute their best and achieve economic progress. This new concept is worthy to be explored by other nations. What every nation ultimately wants is that their people must be happy. Hence, it is time nations followed this concept.

We will be able to live happily in this world when we think each other as human beings first by emphasizing humanity rather than as Indians first, or Americans first. Albert Schweitzer once remarked, "Success is not the key to happiness. Happiness is the key to success. If you love what you are doing, you will be successful." Hence, learn to be happy in your life. Be happy with what you have. Happiness lies in your mind and heart, not in the external materialistic world. You carry nothing when you leave this world. Hence, enjoy every moment to lead a peaceful, happy and joyful life. Add value to you and the people around you.

Happiness in my Personal Life

"Happiness cannot be traveled to, owned, earned, worn or consumed. Happiness is the spiritual experience of living every minute with love, grace, and gratitude." —Denis Waitley

In my personal life, I hardly cared for money although I still belong to a lower-middle-class family. I found most people who believe in making money. But I believe in living happily with my wife with a meager income and resources because I chose to live my life in this way. I am happy at heart because I share my knowledge with the world and I am taking care of my family. I always think of sharing my knowledge free with the world to build a knowledge society. I work very hard from morning to night to share my knowledge free, not to earn money. It landed me into so many financial troubles but I am still happy because I am making a difference. I don't believe in getting into the rat race. I live for eternity, not today.

Enlightened Leadership

"Enlightened leadership is spiritual if we understand spirituality not as some kind of religious dogma or ideology but as the domain of awareness where we experience values like truth, goodness, beauty, love, and compassion, and also intuition, creativity, insight and focused attention." — Deepak Chopra

We are living in an imperfect world. Instead of striving to achieve a perfect world, let us strive to achieve an amazing world where people look for similarities, not differences.

To change others, you must change yourself first. To understand others, you must understand yourself first. The world is going to be more complex than what it is today. Embrace uncertainty by building the right attitude. Enjoy every moment of your life by balancing your personal, professional and social life. Don't leave any room for regrets in your life.

Emphasize Spiritual Education

"How people spend their time is considered more important than how they spend their money; how they support each other within their communities is high on the agenda because the knock-on effects are so beneficial: less crime, better care for the elderly and less abled, and a genuine sense of looking out for another." —Gyalwang Drukpa, *Buddhist spiritual leader*

Spiritual education doesn't mean people must forget earning money and take to spiritual life forever. It is to take care of family and responsibilities by catering a part of human life on spiritual values. It makes them lead a balanced life with less emphasis on materialism. It helps people understand the importance of family, and to be responsible for family and society. It helps them provide meaning to their life.

Spiritualism is the need of the world today. There are conflicts globally based on religion, region, nation, ethnicity and race. People are becoming intolerant globally. They must be imparted with spiritual education. It builds amity and goodwill in people. It eliminates anger and hatred. It irons out parochialism and paves the way for broadmindedness. It opens the minds of others. It eliminates the ego and promotes empathy. In fact, the ego is the root of most problems in the world. When people empathize, they forget their ego. Hence, emphasize spiritual education to bring entire humankind into one platform to achieve peace and happiness.

Health First, Education Second, and Wealth Third

"Happiness is not something readymade. It comes from your own actions." —Dalai Lama

As you need food to grow physically, you need spiritual food to grow spiritually. Spiritual diet is mostly related to mental diet, unlike physical diet. It is the way you improve your thoughts and ideas in a spiritual world. With growing intolerance and challenges globally, you must wed spiritualism to live with peace and tranquility and help others live with peace and fraternity.

People often give wrong priorities leading to several challenges. They must learn to balance their personal, professional and social life to provide meaning to their lives. In my personal life, I emphasize health first, education second, and wealth third. Only when you are healthy you will be able to acquire education. When you have both health and education, you can acquire wealth easily.

Emphasize Ethics and Human Values

"There is only one God and He is God to all; therefore it is important that everyone is seen as equal before God." — Mother Teresa

All religions preach and practice non-violence and peaceful co-existence. It is only a few disgruntled elements that are responsible for the present conflicts globally. They incite others to fight in the name of religion, region, nation, ethnicity, and race. It is deplorable to divide people into these lines indeed! It is essential is to preach and practice camaraderie. We must believe that we are humans first and humans last. We all have similar blood of humanity. Blood doesn't discriminate people. When a child is born, he or she doesn't know which religion and nation he or she belongs. At the time of death, people leave either a good reputation or a bad reputation. Hence, emphasize human values, and humanity to leave a better legacy for future generations.

"No one is my enemy, No one is a foreigner, For me, there is no Hindu, no Muslim, With all I am at peace. God within us renders us, Incapable of hate and prejudice." —Guru Nanak

References

Author's Vision 2030: https://professormsraovision2030.blogspot.com

Author's Amazon URL: http://www.amazon.com/M.-S.-Rao/e/B00MB63BKM

Author's LinkedIn: https://in.linkedin.com/in/professormsrao

Author's YouTube: http://www.youtube.com/user/profmsr7

Author's Facebook page: https://www.facebook.com/Professor-MS-Rao-451516514937414/

Author's Company Facebook Page: https://www.facebook.com/MSR-Leadership-Consultants-India-375224215917499/

Author's Instagram: https://www.instagram.com/professormsrao

Author's Blogs:

http://professormsraoguru.blogspot.com

http://professormsrao.blogspot.com

http://profmsr.blogspot.com

"Life is an opportunity, benefit from it.
Life is beauty, admire it.
Life is bliss, taste it.
Life is a dream, realize it.
Life is a challenge, meet it.
Life is a duty, complete it.
Life is a game, play it.
Life is a promise, fulfill it.
Life is sorrow, overcome it.
Life is a song, sing it.

Life is a struggle, accept it.
Life is a tragedy, confront it.
Life is an adventure, dare it.
Life is luck, make it.
Life is too precious, do not destroy it.
Life is life, fight for it." —Mother Teresa

REFERENCES

Author's Vision 2030: https://professormsraovision2030.blogspot.com

Author's Amazon URL: http://www.amazon.com/M.-S.-Rao/e/B00MB63BKM

Author's LinkedIn: https://in.linkedin.com/in/professormsrao

Author's YouTube: http://www.youtube.com/user/profmsr7

Author's Facebook page: https://www.facebook.com/Professor-MS-Rao-451516514937414/

Author's Company Facebook Page: https://www.facebook.com/MSR-Leadership-Consultants-India-375224215917499/

Author's Instagram: https://www.instagram.com/professormsrao

Author's Blogs:

http://professormsraoguru.blogspot.com

http://professormsrao.blogspot.com

http://profmsr.blogspot.com

https://www.amazon.com/Soft-Leadership-Innovative-Negotiation-Prosperity/dp/1628655909

https://www.london.edu/faculty-and-research/lbsr/think-differently-rewire-your-brain#.WIyux1MrLIU

https://www.thoughtco.com/the-enlightenment-of-the-buddha-449789

https://www.monticello.org/site/research-and-collections/jeffersons-gravestone

http://listverse.com/2013/12/24/10-refreshing-stories-rich-people-who-gave-their-fortunes-away/

http://www.billgeorge.org/page/true-north-discover-your-authentic-leadership

http://simplyg.com/lead-others-first-lead-john-c-maxwell/

http://www.andrewcohen.org/andrew/authentic-leadership.asp

http://www.samyoung.co.nz/2015/12/authentic-leaders-and-followers.html

http://citation.allacademic.com/meta/p_mla_apa_research_citation/1/3/7/9/4/pages137941/p137941-6.php

http://www.consciouslifestylemag.com/subconscious-mind-power/

https://www.reference.com/health/difference-between-disease-illness-b69e4a32392e4c5f

http://www.amazon.in/Power-your-Subconscious-Mind/dp/1416511563

https://www.theguardian.com/lifeandstyle/2005/nov/12/healthandwellbeing.features

http://www.worksafe.govt.nz/worksafe/information-guidance/all-guidance-items/stress-and-fatigue-their-impact-on-health-and-safety-in-the-workplace/stress.pdf

http://mentalhealth.fitness/learn-about-your-diagnosis/depression/

http://www.bestlifeonline.com/foods-to-keep-you-young-forever

http://www.shape.com/lifestyle/beauty-style/forever-young-5-ways-beat-clock-life

https://www.entrepreneur.com/slideshow/224215

https://www.entrepreneur.com/slideshow/224215

http://www.bwy.org.uk/newtoyoga

http://www.bwy.org.uk/pdf/BWY_Sheffield_Presentation-Feb13.pdf

http://www.sivananda.org/teachings/fourpaths.html

http://www.health.harvard.edu/mind-and-mood/yoga-for-anxiety-and-depression

https://www.ncbi.nlm.nih.gov/pmc/articles/PMC2997232/

http://timesofindia.indiatimes.com/india/Yoga-is-our-collective-gift-to-humanity-PM-Modi/articleshow/47762520.cms

https://www.unicef.org/education/files/PeaceEducation.pdf

http://peace-education.org.uk/why-education-for-peace-is-important

https://www.amazon.com/Promoting-Peace-Through-International-Law/dp/0198722737

Authentic Leadership: A Self, Leader, and Spiritual Identity Perspective by Karin Klenke International Journal of Leadership Studies, Vol. 3 Iss. 1, 2007, pp. 68-97

© 2007 School of Global Leadership & Entrepreneurship, Regent University ISSN 1554-3145

The Power of your Subconscious Mind by Dr. Joseph Murphy Revised by Dr. Ian McMahan (Simon & Schuster; Re-issue edition, 3 January 2006)

EPILOGUE

"All that we are is the result of what we have thought. The mind is everything. What we think we become." —Buddha

I have authored this book to underscore mindful leadership. If this book helps you lead your life with purpose and meaning, it will have done its job. If you put this book down feeling that you are better equipped to grow as a mindful leader, I feel that my work as an author has been accomplished.

I would appreciate your valuable feedback to make improvements to this book. You may post your feedback at Facebook Page: https://www.facebook.com/pages/Professor-MSRao/451516514937414 or send me an e-mail: profmsr14@gmail.com. I do keynotes and workshops on mindfulness, leadership, mentoring and coaching. Let me know if you need my services to assist in meeting the learning goals of your organization. I enjoy providing consultation on leadership mentoring and executive coaching. I encourage you to follow my blogs: http://professormsraovision2030.blogspot.in, http://profmsr.blogspot.com, http://professormsrao.blogspot.com, and http://professormsraoguru.blogspot.com. These blogs pertain to Learning, Leadership, Mindfulness, Coaching and Executive Education. If you find them interesting, please share the links with your friends as knowledge grows when shared.

You may share your thoughts about *See the Light in You: Acquire Spiritual Powers to Achieve Mindfulness, Wellness, Happiness, and Success* on social media channels including Facebook, Twitter, and

LinkedIn. I would appreciate a review on your blogs, websites, Amazon or other online bookseller sites.

I sincerely hope that you enjoyed reading this book and found it a useful, practical, and applicable book. If you would like to provide copies to your friends, colleagues or employees, I can offer you bulk discounts with a personalized note and my signature.

Thank you for reading *See the Light in You: Acquire Spiritual Powers to Achieve Mindfulness, Wellness, Happiness, and Success.* I wish you great happiness and success, both in your business and in your life.

Sincerely,
Professor M.S. Rao, Ph.D.
Founder, MSR Leadership Consultants India

About the Author

Professor M.S. Rao, Ph.D
International Leadership Guru
Vision 2030: http://professormsraovision2030.
blogspot.com

Professor M.S. Rao, Ph.D. is an international leadership guru who rose from humble origins. He is recognized as one of the world's leading leadership educators, authors, speakers, coaches, consultants, and practitioners. He is a C-Suite advisor and a sought-after keynote speaker globally. He has thirty-eight years of experience in executive coaching and conducts leadership development training programs for various corporate and educational institutions. He brings a strategic eye and long-range vision given his multifaceted professional experience including military, teaching, training, research, consultancy, and philosophy. He coined a new leadership learning tool—Soft Leadership Grid; a leadership training tool—11E Leadership Grid; and an innovative teaching tool—Meka's Method. His areas of interest include executive coaching, executive education, and leadership. He is passionate about serving and making a difference in the lives of others. He trains a new generation of leaders through leadership education and publications. He advocates gender equality globally (#HeForShe). He shares his leadership wisdom freely with the world on his four blogs. His vision is to build one million students as global leaders by 2030.

He is the Father of 'Soft Leadership' and Founder of MSR Leadership Consultants India. He has authored over forty-five books including the award-winning '21 Success Sutras for CEOs'. His book '21 Success Sutras for Leaders' was selected as a Top 10 Leadership Book of the Year—2013 by San Diego University, USA. He is the recipient of the International Coach of the Year 2013 and 'Heart-repreneur® of the Year 2019, USA. He has published more than 250 papers and articles in prestigious international publications including *Leader to Leader, Thunderbird International Business Review, Strategic HR Review, Development and Learning in Organizations, Industrial and Commercial Training, On the Horizon,* and *The Journal of Values-Based Leadership.* He can be reached: profmsr14@gmail.com and additionally maintains four popular blogs including 'Professor M. S. Rao's Vision 2030: One Million Global Leaders' URL: http://professormsraovision2030.blogspot.com.

LIST OF BOOKS PUBLISHED BY THE AUTHOR

1. 21 Success Sutras for CEOs: How Global CEOs Overcome Leadership Challenges in Turbulent Times to Build Good to Great Organizations
2. Secrets of Successful Public Speaking: How to Become a Great Speaker
3. 21 Success Sutras for Leaders
4. Success Tools for CEO Coaches: Be a Learner, Leader and Ladder
5. Smart Leadership: Lessons for Leaders
6. Soft Leadership: Make Others Feel More Important
7. Soft Leadership: An Innovative Leadership Style to Resolve Conflicts Amicably through Soft Skills and Negotiation Skills to Achieve Global Stability, Peace and Prosperity
8. Soft Leadership: Acquire Leadership Ideas and Insights on Visionary, Inspirational and Life Leadership to Stand Out as a Soft Leader Globally
9. Soft Skills: Your Step-by-Step Guide to Overcome Workplace Challenges to Excel as a Leader
10. Soft Skills for Students: Classroom to Corporate
11. Soft Skills: Enhancing Employability
12. Spirit of Indian Youth: Soft Skills for Young Managers
13. Shortlist Your Employer: Acquire Soft Skills to Achieve Your Career and Leadership Success to Excel as a CEO
14. Success Can Be Yours

15. Stand Out! Build a Successful Career and Become a Global Leader
16. Secrets of Your Leadership Success: The 11 Indispensable E's of a Leader
17. Sharpen Your Mind: Acquire Tools to Achieve Your Success
18. Strategies for Improving Your Business Communication: The Book for Leaders to Communicate and Achieve Professional Success
19. Smartness Guide: Success Tools for Students
20. Sage Advice for Students and Educators: Stay Inspired!
21. Soup for Academic Leaders: Acquire Teaching Tools to Achieve Your Academic Leadership Success
22. Spot Your Leadership Style: Build Your Leadership Brand
23. Secrets for Success: Failure is only a Comma, Not a Full Stop
24. Soar Like Eagles! Success Tools for Freshers
25. Student Leaders: Growing From Students To CEOs
26. Success Sutras for Students: Stay Inspired!
27. Striking Stories on Love and Romance: Spread the Message of Love
28. Students: Concerns and Clarifications on Career, Entrepreneurship and Leadership Success
29. Sutras for CEOs: Acquire Leadership Wisdom from Global Leadership Gurus
30. Stay Hungry: Leadership Lessons from Leadership Gurus for Leaders and CEOs
31. Sutras from Management Gurus: Sage Advice for Learners, Leaders and CEOs
32. Stand Out as a Global Leader: Strive for Global Peace and Prosperity to Make a Difference
33. Success Guide: An Inspirational Guide to Excel as a Leader and CEO
34. Sharing Knowledge on Career, Leadership and Success: Improve Your Attitude and Personality to Excel as a Leader
35. Short Stories on Life Leadership: Life is Beautiful!
36. Professor M.S. Rao's Vision 2030: One Million Global Leaders

Making a Positive Difference in the World

If you have been inspired by *See the Light in You: Acquire Spiritual Powers to Achieve Mindfulness, Wellness, Happiness, and Success* and want to help others lead their lives with purpose and meaning and help Professor M. S. Rao to spread spiritualism globally, here are some ways you can do that —

- Gift *See the Light in You* to your friends, family, and colleagues at work.
- Share your thoughts about *See the Light in You* on Twitter, Facebook, in blogs or write a book review.
- Create a spiritual group to work through *See the Light in You* together, sharing spiritualism with others.
- If you are responsible for developing people within your organization, you can invest in copies of this book for all your Leaders, Managers and Teams.

Printed in Great Britain
by Amazon

84679463R00088